BERBERS AND BLACKS

FULA WOMEN WITH GOURDS OF SOUR MILK AND BUTTER

BERBERS AND BLACKS

IMPRESSIONS OF MOROCCO, TIMBUKTU AND THE WESTERN SUDAN

BY

DAVID PRESCOTT BARROWS

ILLUSTRATED

NEGRO UNIVERSITIES PRESS
WESTPORT, CONNECTICUT

Originally published in 1927
by The Century Company, New York and London

Reprinted in 1970 by
Negro Universities Press
A Division of Greenwood Press, Inc.
Westport, Connecticut

Library of Congress Catalogue Card Number 70-129938

SBN 8371-1003-3

Printed in the United States of America

TO MY WIFE

INTRODUCTORY NOTE

The languages spoken by the different peoples of West Africa are notably varied and distinct. This makes intercourse difficult for the traveler, and it seems equally difficult to secure good interpreters, but one can easily assembly a list of phrases—Wolof, Bambara or "Djoula" (trade speech),—which will be generally understood in the Sudan, and which enable him to secure essential supplies and information and to exercise a kind of command over his company. In northern Nigeria the Hausa language prevails, and from excellent manuals of this tongue, the traveler can obtain enough phrases to make his primary wants known.

African place names, as transliterated by the several European nations,—Portuguese, Spanish, English, Dutch, and French,—exhibit numerous variations and some inaccuracies. It is difficult to follow a consistent plan. For relatively obscure localities, it seems wise to follow the spelling determined upon by the nation politically dominant, even though its orthography may be very different from our own. Ouargla might be clearer to the English reader if spelled "Wargla," and Ouagadougou if spelled "Wagadugu," but for such places as these the spellings laid down on French maps will eventually come to prevail, and it seems better for another nation to familiarize itself with the authorized form of the word than to further complicate the matter by substitutes of its own.

On the other hand, there are some words which have been current so long in our language, and have become so fixed in our literature, albeit in a corrupted form, that, at least for the present, it is impracticable to revise them. For this reason, I have written the name of the famous Saharan city, "Timbuktu," even though this spelling perpetuates an error. The word is actually pronounced Tom-boúk-too, with the accent on the second syllable, and the modern French spelling, "Tombouctou," is quite exact. I leave it, however, as the English-reading eye might expect to find it. Modern English books have now quite generally substituted "Sudan" for Soudan, and as this land lies under British sovereignty as well as French, I have followed the English spelling. It is more common for us to print "Ivory Coast" than Côte d'Ivoire, but if reference is to the French colony and not to the fringe of the African shore, I think the French spelling should be followed.

These illustrations will prepare the reader for inconsistencies throughout the book, but I have tried, with few exceptions, to spell and accent place names in such a way that if spoken they reproduce the pronunciation locally recognized.

I am under obligation which no words can express or repay for encouragement and help on this journey. I cannot give the names of all who befriended me,

but they include officials in the governments of Great
Britain, France, and Belgium, soldiers and colonial
servants whose lives have given order to Africa, and
added luster to their nations' flags, local administrators and residents throughout the countries I journeyed
in. I feel deepest gratitude for their interest, helpful-
ness, and hospitality.

It was not men alone, however, whose kindliness
brightened this travel. Since the World War, French
women have commenced to accompany their husbands
to Africa. In isolated and lonely posts they have organized their *ménages,* using the poor facilities of their remote stations to establish French domesticity and
charm of living. I was a swiftly passing guest in such
homes between Timbuktu and the Côte d'Ivoire, and
I pay my tribute to the service these true heroines
render to their families and to their country. Durable
empire cannot be built by men alone. Less than half
of the contribution that advanced societies may make
to backward peoples is represented when men go unac-
companied by women. A camp of soldiers is the most
impermanent of influences. A solitary man may bring
temporary order to a troubled district. But only homes
conserve the fruits of labor, and by building their
materials into other homes improve society. The great
service that women render is to select and preserve that
limited part of man's diverse operations that has social
value. One sees this in colonial life, where contrasts
are great, where all sorts of things are undertaken, but
where it is so difficult to establish the work of men's
hands.

There is a notable literature on the region covered
by this book. I cite a few works only.

Mungo Park: Travels in the Interior of Africa, 1799.
This is obtainable in the inexpensive edition of
Everyman's Library. Also, Journal of a Mission
Into Africa, 1805. London, 1815.

René Caillié: Journal d'un Voyage á Temboctou et
á Jenné, dans L'Afrique Centrale. Three volumes.
Paris, 1830.

Henry Barth: Travels and Discoveries in North and
Central Africa. Three volumes. New York, 1857.

Oskar Lenz: Timbuktu, Reise durch Marokko, die
Sahara und den Sudan. Two volumes. Leipzig, 1884.

Charles de Foucauld: Reconnaissance au Maroc.
Paris, 1888.

Félix Dubois: Timbuctoo, The Mysterious. Translated from the French. London, 1897. Also, Dubois: Notre Beau Niger. Paris, 1911.

E. F. Gautier: La Conquête du Sahara, Paris, 1919;
Le Sahara, Paris, 1923; The Trans-Saharan Railway, in the Geographical Review, January, 1925.

Georges-Marie Harrdt and Louis Audouin-Dubreuil:
La Prémière Traversée du Sahara en Automobile.

The French official reports, Protectorat Français
au Maroc; Annuaire Économique et Financier,
1921-1922; La Renaissance du Maroc; Dix Ans
de Protectorat, 1922; and Annuaire du Gouvern-
ment Général de L'Afrique Occidental Française,
1922, are full of exact geographic, political and
economic information.

A good many volumes have been published by explorers, officers and missionaries who have made studies of the peoples of the Sudan. These works, which can not be cited here, disclose a rich ethnological field in which much waits to be done. That part of the western Sudan lying in Northern Nigeria is well described in works by British authors. I cite only two: Lady Lugard's "Tropical Dependency," London, 1905, and General Sir Frederick Lugard's "Dual Mandate in Tropical Africa," London, 1922, an authoritative exposition of the principles of colonial administration.

The illustrations in this volume are from snapshots made by the author. The sketch maps have been prepared by the author from a considerable collection of maps, reports and recent geographical information.

The *Service Géographique* of French West Africa produces maps of all the colonies, which show physiographic features, routes, political subdivisions, and the distribution of native stocks. I found the map of Africa, by A. Taride, Paris, scale 1:8,000,000, an excellent travel guide. It has all places of importance correctly located, and I recommend it as an easily obtainable basis for studies of this region.

DAVID P. BARROWS.

The University of California,
December, 1926.

CONTENTS

ILLUSTRATIONS

MAPS

BERBERS AND BLACKS

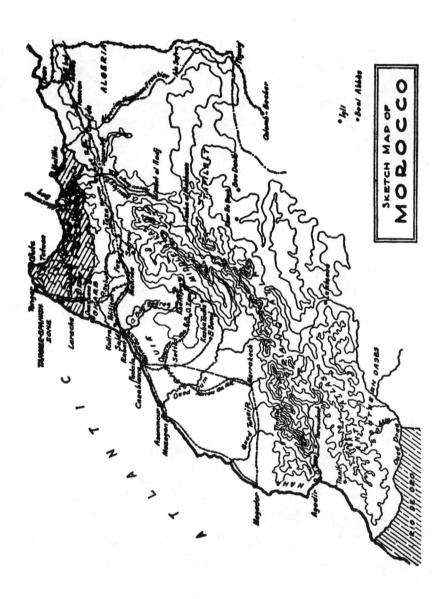

SKETCH MAP OF
MOROCCO

CHAPTER I

THE SPELL

THE spell of the unknown interior of a continent is a lure fatal to man's ease and safety. That spell once cast can not be resisted. The desire to go where the way is forbidden, to penetrate regions where rumor and tradition have created undiscovered wonders to be the first to bring back knowledge of a remote and mysterious kingdom, has incited men of our race to prodigious adventures.

The last continental mystery was Africa. European knowledge began with the coast line, and at this point exploration was long arrested. The Portuguese began the exploration of the African coast half a century before the first voyage of Columbus. Eventually they rounded Africa and reached India and Malaysia. The line of their fortresses and trading settlements, which surrounds the continent from Mazagan to Mozambique, was completely drawn more than four hundred years ago. But in spite of their activity, and that of their European rivals who followed them, the interior of the continent remained unpenetrated and almost unknown.

In 1795 a young Scotchman, Mungo Park, landed on the river Gambia, and broke the way into the interior. He was at this time twenty-four years old. His

physical and moral powers may be judged from what
he accomplished, and from the manner of his death.
He was entering Africa with the support of a British
society, the Association for Promoting the Discovery
of Africa. Alone and single-handed, the constant victim
of hunger, fever, and native brutality, Park traversed
the interior of Senegal, the desertic south-Saharan region of Kaarta, where he was robbed and imprisoned
by the Moors, and, after many months of persistence,
he discovered what he had been bidden to find. It was
known to Europe that a great river traversed the interior of this part of Africa, a river known as the
"Joliba" or the "Niger," but no European had ever
seen its waters and both its sources and its mouth were
unknown. On the 20th of July, having escaped from the
bondage of the Moors, destitute and weak from his
sufferings, Park reached the valley of this river at
Ségou, the capital of the Bambara Kingdom.

"I saw with infinite pleasure", he wrote, "the great
object of my mission—the long sought for majestic
Niger, glittering to the morning sun. . . . and flowing
slowly *to the eastward.*"

He descended the Niger about eighty miles, and
then, completely exhausted and without resources,
turned reluctantly westward, and struggled through
the Fouta Djallon mountains to the coast. He had long
been given up for dead.

He returned to this quest for the true course of the
Niger in 1805, and again entered the interior with a
party of forty-four Europeans, including his brother-
in-law, Alexander Anderson, and a guard of British

soldiers. Death assailed them as they progressed, and on reaching the Niger at Bamako only eleven Europeans remained alive. This number had been reduced to five, one of whom had gone mad, when, on the 19th of November, resolved to follow the Niger to its mouth, he embarked the survivors of his party on a craft which he had constructed by lashing together two native canoes. To the Colonial Office he wrote:

"I shall set sail for the east with the fixed resolution to discover the termination of the Niger or perish in the attempt. . . . Though all the Europeans who are with me should die, and though I were myself half dead, I would still persevere, and if I could not succeed in the object of my journey I would at least die on the Niger."

To his wife he wrote: "It grieves me to the heart to write anything that may give you uneasiness; but such is the will of Him who doeth all things well! Your brother Alexander, my dear friend, is no more! He died of the fever at Sansanding on the morning of the 28th of October. I am afraid that, impressed with a woman's sense and the anxieties of a wife, you may be led to consider my situation as a great deal worse than it is. . . . We have already embarked all our things and shall sail the moment I have finished this letter. I do not intend to stop or land anywhere till we reach the coast; which I suppose will be some time in the end of January."

This was the last communication ever received from Park. He embarked on the river, believing it to be the upper course of the Congo. He was ignorant of the

great rapids that make the Niger un-navigable between
the middle and lower stretches. He and his companions
lost their lives in the Bussa Rapids, north of Jebba.

While Park and his companions were thus the first
Europeans ever to traverse the main course of the
Niger, it is not probable that they saw, or even approached, the other object of their exploration,—the
famed city of Timbuktu. For this place lies in the
desert some miles north of the Niger, and at the time
Park passed this point hostilities between him and the
natives were incessant, and a landing was impossible.

The first European to make an authentic visit to
Timbuktu was the Scotch explorer Major Alexander
Laing. Laing crossed the Sahara from Tripoli in 1826,
and was murdered near Timbuktu on the 26th of September of the same year. He was followed by the remarkable young French adventurer, René Caillié, who,
after years of waiting and preparation, by pretending
to be a Mohammedan native of Egypt, reached the
city in 1828, and, accompanying a caravan across the
desert to Morocco, regained France.

Between his time and the final capture of Timbuktu
by the French, only two other explorers reached this
region and city. The first was Heinrich Barth, a German in the employ of the British government, who
crossed the Sahara from Tripoli to Lake Chad in 1850,
and after the death of his companions in that vicinity,
continued alone, and reached Timbuktu in September
1853. Here he was detained many months, but eventually escaped and regained the Mediterranean by the
route over which he had entered Central Africa. The

other was an Austrian, Dr. Oskar Lenz, who reached Timbuktu by way of Morocco in 1879.

Astonishing though it seems,—so long was the development of Africa postponed,—one hundred years passed after the time of Park's discovery of the Niger before the French conquered the Sudan, and permanently occupied the city of Timbuktu. The occupying force was led by Joffre, then a colonel in the French Colonial Army, now a Marshal of France, with fame secured for all time by the Victory of the Marne. The valley of the great river and the far vaster region which it in part traverses are now well known, explored, conquered, and organized. The mystery that lured Park and those who followed him is no longer a mystery. An immense and promising domain has been disclosed, lying between the Sahara and the tropical forest of the Guinea coast and the Congo. Yet our civilization still hugs the shore line, and the long period when the interior of the continent was unpenetrated is reflected in the terminology of Western Africa which continues to describe the country by sections of its shore, the "Barbary Coast", the "Grain Coast", the "Ivory Coast", the "Gold Coast", the "Slave Coast", the "Oil Coast" The general designation for Western Africa seems to be simply "The Coast", and the white men who carry on their part in its dangerous and forbidding life are still known as "Coasters".

Even the most experienced of these European coast residents and traders rarely display knowledge of the interior. They live in little shabby settlements, where whites and blacks commingle, built on low bluffs or on sandy bars that stretch along the unhealthy African rim. Harbors are few. The great swell of the Atlantic is always rolling in, breaking and leaping upon the shore. Behind these sandy fringes of the continent, lie long brilliant lagoons, and behind these, magnificent but pestilential tropical forests which, to a depth of 100 to 140 miles, stretch the entire length of the West Coast below Senegambia, until they merge into the equatorial forest of the Congo.

Except along a few streams navigable to small ships, the Coasters have preferred to abide on the shores where enterprise planted them four hundred and fifty years ago, while the interior remained through the centuries under the control of native sovereignties, ravished by native barbarism made predatory by disturbances set on foot by the traffic of the shore line.

This condition is certain now to change. Between the barriers of the Sahara Desert on the one hand, and the tropical wilderness on the other, is a magnificent interior which extends across Africa, from Senegal to Abyssinia. It is inhabited by some forty millions of people. It has been, and still is, the seat of native kingdoms and empires of no mean attainments. Here native African culture appears to have reached its highest point. This advancement, amounting to genuine civilization, is represented not only in the political organizations which make its history, but in numerous cities defended by great walls, filled with temples, palaces, schools, and markets, supporting manufactures, and giving facilities for a commerce that

extends by diverging caravan routes as far as Egypt
and the Mediterranean.

This broad belt is known as the "Sudan". We get
the word from the Arabic, *Bilad es Sudan*—the "Land
of the Blacks". The people *are* blacks, but they are
not the true negroes of the African forest. They are a
negroid or mulatto population, formed by the mingling
of numerous streams of blood. In some cases they are
predominately white. The character and the prospects
of these peoples, as they appear to a traveler, will be
described in this narrative.

The Sudan is divided, at about its center, into
easterly and westerly portions by the great interior
sea called Lake Chad, although this body of water, and
the fertile lands which surround it, is rather a central
point of Sudanese culture than a line of demarcation.
The Eastern Sudan, with the exception of the western
portion nearest to Lake Chad, is familiar to British
and American readers through the Egyptian conquest
under Khedive Ismaïl, the Mahdist Rebellion, the
death of Gordon at Khartum, and the British re-con-
quest under Kitchener in 1898. There has been less
realization that this zone of Sudanese culture extends
westward, quite across Africa, until it merges in the
native life of Senegambia on the Atlantic Coast, and
that the great proportion of population, the most
famous cities, and the most highly developed culture,
lie in the region west of Lake Chad. The interest of
this region to the student is the fact that it is still
practically unaffected by Europe. Mohammedanism

penetrated here centuries ago, and the spirit and institutions of Islam have contributed to make it what it is, but its culture is as yet unaffected by European influence. While it has now been brought firmly under French and British authority, the population of Europe is most sparsely represented. Its recent exploration and conquest have been achieved by a mere handful of white men, relying upon the devotion of the black soldiers who followed them. It is governed in the same manner.

Centuries ago, coincident with, but also anticipating, the influence of Islam, native states arose in the Sudan —emirates, kingdoms and empires—built up by the vigor of native princes and their militant followers. The boundaries of these states expanded and relaxed as fortune shifted, but one succeeded another in keeping alive the spirit of empire and domination. The native cities that arose between Lake Chad and the upper course of the Niger, comprise scores of famous communities such as Kano, Sokoto, Goa, Djenné, Ségou, Timbuktu. Amidst the hundreds of such cities that have risen and fallen, many still thrive or are again reviving. While by no means the largest, circumstances contributed to make the name of one well-known to all readers,—Timbuktu.

Today a voyage to Timbuktu presents small dangers and few difficulties. Yet few make the journey, outside of that small number dispatched to the region as soldiers or administrators of the French Republic, and popularly Timbuktu appears to remain in the region of mystery and unreality.

This narrative comprises the record of a holiday trip to Timbuktu, and a part of the world little known and under-appreciated. In 1923 I found myself, for the first time in my life, with prospects of an extended vacation. Several reasons determined me to spend a part of this time in Africa. For years Timbuktu had been in my mind, but there were other considerations. I had seen something of the interior of the other continents, but nothing of Africa. I had spent ten years of life in the colonial administration of the United States, but had seen little of French colonial government; and France is today the greatest of Africa's colonizing powers. Some thirteen millions of the citizens of the United States, and several more millions of the inhabitants of the West Indies, are derived from the black populations of western Africa. I felt a curiosity to visit the African home of this race, to see its culture at first hand, and so, perhaps, better appreciate the development of the African race in America. Finally, I longed to reach again a vast and spacious region where human life, though prosperous and flourishing, is organized on simple and primitive lines, where contact with the activities of Europe and America an be broken temporarily, and where one may regain the sense of resourcefulness, of freedom, and of repose which our western civilization too frequently denies. These considerations settled my decision. I can record that in all that I sought I was disappointed in nothing. The months spent in the Sudan count among the most enjoyable and rewarding I have ever known.

But to understand the history and the prospects of
the Sudan, one must see the land of the Berbers and at
least glimpse the fringe of the vast desert of the
Sahara—the sea of sand which both separates and
unites the north of Africa with the regions of the
Senegal and the Niger. The Berbers have been a
dominant factor in the Sudan, and the empire of
Morocco extended to Senegal. In 1591 an expedition
of 4,000 soldiers, many of them renegades from Andalucía, followed by a convoy of 8,000 camels, crossed
the Sahara from southern Morocco and captured Timbuktu. The Berbers have always drawn upon the
Sudan for man-power, for black slaves and black
soldiers. The commerce of Marrakech and Mogador is
linked with the trans-Saharan trade. Clearly, a study
of the Sudan must begin with Morocco.

Morocco remained for centuries a region closed
against European observation. Within the last few
years it has been opened, subdued, set in order. Except along a few lines of caravan travel, the Sahara
was unknown to Europeans until twenty-five years ago.
Today its exploration nears completion. Again, in this
part of Africa the spell of the unrevealed and the forbidding awoke the unconquerable curiosity of our race.
Men offered themselves to go and explore within these
forbidden frontiers. The motives that inspired Mungo
Park may be illustrated by another example.

I was wandering one evening at dusk on the outskirts of the modern city of Casablanca, and came
upon a recently-reared monument which bears the following inscription:

A la Mémoire de
Charles de Foucauld
Explorateur du Maroc
1883-84
Officier Explorateur Prête
Apôtre du Sahara
Mort pour la France
à Tamanrasset (Hoggar)
le 1ère Décembre 1916

Charles de Foucauld—the name awoke vague recollections; the inscription stimulated inquiry. His life has been eloquently and sympathetically described by a member of the French Academy, M. René Bazin (*Charles de Foucauld, Explorateur du Maroc, Ermite au Sahara, Paris 1921*). He was a son of a family of the old French nobility, born in 1858, the grandson of a retired army officer. He was educated at the military school of St. Cyr and at the cavalry school of Saumur. In 1880 he was sent with his regiment, the 4th Huzzars, to Africa. This regiment became the famous 4th Chasseurs d'Afrique. He took part with his regiment against the insurrection that occurred in South Oran in 1881. This campaign fixed in his character the major interests of his life—the desert and Morocco. He resolved to penetrate the latter country, at that time closed, defiant, hostile, but destined, as he saw, to pass under the domination óf France. To gain freedom for his enterprise, he resigned from the Army, and in June, 1883, at the age of twenty-five, he left Algiers to undertake the exploration that was to make him famous.

He traveled, disguised as a Jew, in the company of
a Jewish rabbi named Mardochée, who was a native of
the oasis of Akka, in the extreme south of Morocco,
and who is said to have been the first Jew ever to establish himself as a merchant at Timbuktu. His exploration lasted a year. He traveled from Tangier
to Fez and Taza, and then, at great peril and as the
protégé of powerful chieftains whose protection he
purchased, he traveled southward, through forbidden
districts of the Atlas, to the south Moroccan valleys of
the Sous and the Draa. He carried his scientific instruments wrapped in his clothing. His disguise was
penetrated, but, happily, by Moors expectant and even
hopeful of French intervention. He endured the hard-
ships and indignities which a traveler of his assumed
race was due to receive. The courage and endurance of
his Jewish companion failed him; but Foucauld
remained tenacious and unrelenting in his persistence.
Reaching Mogador, where was a French consulate, he
replenished his means and turned back to traverse the
entire southern circle of the Atlas Mountains, following the Moulouya River down to the Algerian frontier.
His publication, *Reconnaissance au Maroc,* was the
first accurate, modern revelation of the country he had
set himself to penetrate.

His family had been notable for religious piety,
and for the leaders which it had furnished to the
French church. He himself, at this age, was a skeptic,
following the mode of life of young men of his class.
But the mystical enthusiasm which lay at the bottom
of his character asserted itself. He professed conver-

sion, renounced his military profession, and in January, 1890, entered the Trappist Monastery of Notre-Dame-des-Neiges. He served as an initiate of the order in Palestine, returned to France, was ordained priest, and, accomplishing the object which had grown upon his mind and come to dominate his religious purposes, obtained approval to establish himself as a missionary in the Sahara.

Descending from the southern slopes of the Atlas range near the frontier between Morocco and Algeria, is a great "fossil river", which, in Quarternary times, fertilized and enriched with its perennial flow this now arid region. This is the famous Oued Saoura. The gradual desiccation of the desert has reduced this river to a great "wash" which traverses the desert for hundreds of miles. Flowing water appears in its channel only intermittently, but underneath its sands the drainage of the Atlas seeps, and, through wells and tunnels, water is brought to the surface, and gives rise to a long chain of oases that end at Insalah, the nearest approach to the central mountain mass of the Ahaggar. The palm groves, while not continuous along this dead stream, nevertheless justify its description as a ribbon of verdure, three hundred and seventy-five miles long and a hundred yards wide.

Beni-Abbes is a little settlement on this line of oases. In 1900 it was an outpost in the French penetration of the Sahara, and served as a center from which the exploration and pacification of the desert were achieved. Here Foucauld established himself and built a primitive hermitage.

In July, 1901, Henri Laperrine was appointed *Commandant Supérieur* of the Saharan oases. The French conquest of the Sahara centers around this redoubtable and heroic soldier. He organized the corps of desert camel-soldiers, the *meharistes*. He trained himself and his officers in the technique of desert exploration. By a policy of resolute action and conciliation, he pacified the Tuareg and suppressed the desert marauders. From 1880, when he began his African experience as a young cavalry officer, until his death on the desert by the crash of an airplane in 1920, Laperrine's life was devoted to the solution of the Sahara. Two years younger than the Viscount de Foucauld, Laperrine had been trained in the same schools, and had served in the same regiment. Their friendship was renewed at Beni-Abbes, and they remained close friends and co-workers to the end.

A crisis in the military situation during these years illustrates the history of Saharan conquest, and what Foucauld sought to contribute thereto. In 1903, an immense "harka", counting 6,000 combatants, was organized in the Moroccan region of Tafilelt by one of the most persistent enemies of the French—Mouley Mustapha, Sherif of Matrara. On August 17th this harka fell furiously upon the oasis post of Taghit, defended by a French garrison of 470 men, commanded by Captain Susbielle. The defense by this garrison during the 18th, 19th, and 20th of August, ranks among the most magnificent feats of the French army of Africa. The desperate situation of the garrison was relieved by a mounted company of the Foreign Legion under Lieutenant Pointurier, and by a mounted detachment led from Beni-Abbes by Lieutenant Delachaux. The harka, which had sustained 1,200 casualties, abandoned its attack on Taghit. But on the 2nd of September it fell upon a mounted platoon of the 2nd regiment of the Foreign Legion, and in its first charge killed or wounded the two officers of the company, all the non-commissioned officers, and a large part of the men. The survivors grouped themselves in the sand about their dead to fight to the last. Two mounted spahis escaped through the cordon of enemies, and carried the alarm to Taghit. The relief party rescued the survivors—some thirty men, commanded by a twice wounded soldier—the supply-sergeant, Tisserant.

Foucauld, to carry assistance to these wounded, and to exercise his office as a priest, traversed, in twenty-four hours, and quite alone, the 120 kilometers which separate Beni-Abbes from Taghit. For the twenty-four succeeding days, he remained at the side of these stricken men without once availing himself of the bed which was provided him.

The year following, Foucauld abandoned his hermitage at Beni-Abbes for more advanced posts in the desert, and finally settled at Tamanrasset, the western portal to the Ahaggar Mountains. Here he remained, a solitary, spiritual influence in this vast region, an enthusiastic supporter of French aims, a diligent student of the language and customs of the Tuareg, until his assassination at the end of 1916.

At Tamanrasset, the central point of the Sahara, the bodies of Foucauld and Laperrine lie entombed together.

A judgment of the lives of two men such as these is beyond the intent of this notice. I have sketched their careers to emphasize the motives behind imperial expansion. Men of our day, as of past ages, do not act exclusively from calculations of personal advantage. With men of a certain type, the strongest incentives are the bonds of discipline, the obedience to the spirit of their corps and profession, the profound satisfactions afforded by self-sacrifice, the gratification that comes from opposing their courage and endurance to the hardest tests, the pity roused in them by spectacles of misery, cruelty, and disorder which superior morality and organization may redress, the enthusiasm for the prestige and glory of country. It is men affected by such feelings who have built up modern colonial empires. It is the fashion of current writers to attribute imperial expansion to the insistence of the money power, to the avaricious incitement of capitalism. Such explanations are part of the general theory that all human history is capable of an economic interpretation. Such theories do not explain the lives of Laperrine and Foucauld.

In the history of the modern conquest of Africa, commercialism has followed gingerly in the steps of the empire builder. Governments have frequently deplored the enterprise of their colonial servants; have repudiated their work and accepted with reluctance the increased responsibilities created by the restlessness of

men on the ground. These latter men, it is true, have
been few in number; their character may be exceptional or eccentric, yet they must be taken into
consideration, because to them is due the transformation of Africa. And it is the exceptional men, who are
not governed by ordinary motives, and who do not
pursue ordinary tasks, that are of interest. I take it
that what we want to know about the human race is
the extreme limit of its capabilities—physical, intellectual, moral. What is the utmost that it can achieve
by resolution and self-sacrifice? If so, it is the exceptional performance that justifies study.

The modern spirit of internationalism opposes itself
to the spirit of patriotism, and to the extension of
European and American dominion. It does not offer
alternatives to the control of the world by the forces
of our civilization, but it attacks that control. But its
attacks and its opposition seem impotent against the
devotion of a few men to whom the triumph of our
civilization has become a religion, and who ask nothing
for themselves but the opportunity to advance that
triumph in the hard and savage places of the earth.

CHAPTER II

BARBARY is an ancient name for the north coast of Africa, from Egypt all the way round the shore to where the southwestern limits of the Atlas Mountains reach the sea. The word is perhaps more familiar when used descriptively as "Barbary Pirates" and "Barbary Coast". San Francisco had its Barbary Coast in the days before the great fire, while Barbary Pirates still evoke tales among seafaring men. There is an old toast or "grog tot" still lingering in the American Navy, from the times of Decatur and Bainbridge, that devotes to the punishment of God the "bar*bay*rious Moors". Barbary is, by nature, a European frontier. Here, long ago, were the famous colonies of Phoenicians and Romans. Here St. Augustine exercised his office as a Christian bishop and wrote the *Civitas Dei*. Then North Africa was separated from its European associations by Semitic invasions, and the enduring antipathies of religious hostility. Only in recent years has Europe re-asserted its interest in this region, and in its reunion to western civilization. France is the instrument of this conquest and regeneration.

The population of the Barbary Coast is one of the most mixed in the world, but back of the ports and cities which fringe the rugged coast-line are plains, plateaus, and mountains which, from time immemorial, have been held by a single race—the race which gives its name to the land—the Berbers. Setting out to visit the South Saharan region of the Sudan, the "Land of the Blacks", I found that conditions in that great African zone were unintelligible without reference to the Berbers. The fortunes of the white race of North Africa and the black race of the Niger have been commingled for centuries. Under the control of France, these two races are now united in the bonds of a vast empire. They will work together toward ends established by a European control. They form the human material out of which is being organized the man-power of a new French state.

It is the customary thing to apply the name "Arab" to peoples whom we see following camels, dwelling in tents, and wearing the flowing garments of the East. This, in North Africa, leads to an over-emphasis of the part the Arab race takes in the population of the country. The land is Arabic in its religion, and in many of the more obvious aspects of its life. But probably only a minor part of the population are descendants of Arabia. There was an old white stock here long before the arrival of migrations from the eastern shores of the Mediterranean, and this stock is the Berber. It appears to predominate everywhere. It maintains, in its hill settlements, its ancient purity of physical type which is that of a pure white race.

Outside the cities, the Berbers are divided between two modes of life—the nomadic and the sedentary. The broad plains that lie back from the coast, like the higher plateaus, are capable of extensive agricultural production. The soil is reported excellent, but the absence or irregularity of water-supply, and the strife between tribes, have worked against the building up of farming and horticultural communities on these plains. The population depends, primarily, on its flocks of sheep and its herds of cattle and camels. The settlement is a camp, either of low black tents, called "douars", or of rough huts of earth and branches called "noualas". These transient homes are grouped in circles and in this way amid the dwellings is formed a corral where the animals are gathered at night for protection.

Sedentary life belongs to the hills where struggle for subsistence has compelled the Berbers to terrace the slopes and gorges, to plant orchards of olives, figs, peaches, and pears, to practice irrigation, and thus become fixed to the soil. In such stabilized sites, villages appear. The houses are built of adobe, rarely of stone. The villages themselves are compact communities, governed by customs that have not altered for centuries.

The anarchistic condition of the country, the lawlessness which has ever swept the land, have compelled the creation of another type of dwelling—the "kasbah" or fortress. These are high walled, battlemented strong points, placed on lofty defendable ground or ridges, and are the abodes of chieftains, to whom the less powerful resort for protection.

Since the Arabian conquest of North Africa, twelve hundred years ago, these Berber peoples have made profession of Islam; nominally, at least, they are Mohammedan. But they have never submitted themselves to the law of the Koran, holding stiffly to ancient customs which regulate their domestic relations, inheritance, and rights to property. They have never admitted into their communities the "kadis", whose function it is to expound the law of Mohammed, and to judge according to the Koran.

The spirit of Mohammedanism is arbitrary, aristocratic. It gives rise to strong autocratic governments. But the Berbers are by nature independents, anarchists, democrats. Their tribes are family associations. Their villages are little popular states where affairs are settled by the *djemaa* or council of all the men. Unions and confederacies are not unknown, but the tendency is for each small community to retain its isolation and independence whenever superior authority is relaxed.

While the nomadic tribes were first described as "Arabs", and thought of as a distinct race of men, increased familiarity with the Berbers shows that there is no hard and fast line of stock or race between the herdsmen of the camps and the grain growers and orchard cultivators of the villages. The two kinds of life merge, but the wandering life with the herds is preferred, because it has afforded greater independence, larger opportunity for military prowess, and, under the prevailing condition of things, greater affluence.

In traversing Morocco, or the plateau country of Algeria there is another object that constantly meets the eye. This is the shrine or "koubba", the grave of a holy man, a saint, a mahdi, a "marabout". These koubbas are small square buildings surmounted by low domes, and entered through horseshoe-arch doorways. They are everywhere—on hillside, eminence, and plain. They are the monuments of the real religion of the country which is a worship of local saints and heroes, but such shrines have an important social influence, fixing the points of reunion and intercourse between communities and tribes and even giving rise to towns and sanctuaries, or *zaouias,* like the Biblical "cities of refuge."

In a country in which rainfall is seasonal, and the water supply unreservoired, every fountain or spring is precious, and these springs, called *ain* in Arabic or Berber, give names to hundreds of localities. About a spring, there may develop a market place, where, on a certain day of the week, the tribesmen and villagers meet for exchange of produce and manufactures. In the course of time, such spots become sanctified by shrines.

The life of this Berber race is thus necessarily simple, austere, conservative. Their anarchistic propensities, however, have not prevented their being united again and again, through the power of religious revival, to reform the rule of the land or to drive back the foreign aggressor. The history of Morocco is the history of such religious movements, having warfare as a method, and the subversion of decadent dynasties as an objective. The strange thing in the history of Northwestern Africa is that these cyclonic tempests of religious fanaticism have always come from the desert or from south of the Atlas. By such tempests the spirit of Morocco was raised again and again for the conquest of North Africa and the Spanish peninsula.

The cities of Barbary have a life of their own. Each owes its foundation to a new conqueror of the land. They are new institutions when contrasted with the ancient tribal camps and mountain villages, and they are not purely Berber but cosmopolitan in population. They did not rise to their full magnificence of bastioned walls and gates, of luxurious palaces, of mosques and towers until the expelled Moors from Spain carried back into Africa the cultured city life, which had been developed to such stately proportions at Córdoba, Sevilla, and Granada.

If one wishes to-day to study the Berbers, he must visit both Algeria and Morocco, and then he must be transported far into the south, along the valleys of the Senegal and the Niger, which represent the southern limits of Berber expansion. Furthermore, America is not fully intelligible until one has seen Barbary. The life of the larger part of the New World is full of arts, institutions, and terms of speech that have been brought from Africa by way of Spain.

With my mind well occupied with this problem of the diffusion of life and culture, I spent the month of October, 1923, in Spain. Here the firm impress of the Berber remains. The Catholic kings battled long and relentlessly to extinguish the roots of African culture. Yet Spanish civilization is as truly based on Africa as Russian civilization is on Asia.

More than once in Andalucía men of social position and enlightened views summed up the characteristics of their life by saying, "*Sómos Árabes*".

I spent most of November and December in Algeria and Morocco, but I passed through the first country hurriedly, my mind fixed on an early departure for West Africa. I have as memories of Algeria only the experiences of a few days. The country recalls California. It has the same rugged face set toward a brilliant sea. Similar valleys are separated by low hills from the coast. It has a great mountain range that divides the fruitful land from great desert spaces, just as the Sierras separate western California from the Colorado Desert and the Mohave.

The comparison is less striking when one compares French achievement in Algeria with American achievement in California. At first sight, the advantage would seem to have lain with the former project—far greater proximity to the source of colonization, twenty years priority in point of time. But these factors have been outweighed by others—the indisposition of the French people to expand to new homes, the numbers and resistant qualities of the Algerians and Berbers, and also differences in the political systems under which the two regions have been colonized by European stock. California was seized and settled at one bound. Its American settlers waited on nothing. Consider the political aggressiveness of those men who organized themselves as a state, gave themselves a constitution, and demanded admission to the American Union within twenty-two months after the cession of California by

Mexico. There is no parallel to this anywhere in the history of European imperial expansion. Algeria has been a French possession for nearly a hundred years. Everything has been done, that it is practical to do, to add this country to the territory of France, to encourage the settlement of French colonists, to assimilate the status of the natives in that of French citizenship. The work done seems admirable, but progress has been slow. Even to-day, the land does not suggest France. The Berber type predominates everywhere. Other nationalities than the French, particularly Spaniards and Italians, have come as settlers in such numbers as to somewhat disquiet the proponents of colonization. The little French towns of Algeria are seemingly prosperous, attractive and orderly, but they give no evidence of the prodigious enterprise, nor of the boundless resources that have built up the communities of California.

I had a charming visit with American friends at the little commune of St. Aimé. The gentleman is a geologist, and was employed as an expert in the petroleum explorations of British oil interests associated with the name of Lord Cowdray. His wife is a former student of the University of California. These friends took me on a beautiful automobile trip into the hills back of the plain. We visited Berber villages set in the defiles of the mountains, and reached the inland town of Mascara, where the railroad from Oran passes through the Atlas to the desert oases of Figuig and Colomb-Bechar. The main line of the railroad carried me on through the garrisoned town of Sidi-bel-Abbés, the headquarters of the Foreign Legion in Africa, to the city of Tlemcen, near the Algerian-Morocco frontier.

No visitor to Algeria should fail to visit Tlemcen, for it is a truly Berber city of great interest, set in surroundings of surpassing beauty, and due to the long presence here of the French, it is more open to examination than are comparable cities of Morocco. Centuries ago there was a Roman camp here, around which grew up a town which has left various stone remains bearing Latin inscriptions of the Christian period. Then, at the end of the seventh century, came the Arabs, and finally Tlemcen became the capital of Central Morocco. The Almoravides and Almohades who ruled Spain from Córdoba and Granada favored this place, and its finest existent buildings are of the same date as the Alhambra, but the "Grand Mosque" is earlier, of the twelfth century. At the end of the middle ages Tlemcen was a famous city, supposed to have 125,000 inhabitants, and it was then the center of trade between Africa and countries of the Mediterranean. Only persistent fighting by the French gave them possession of this place, their final occupation dating from 1842. Today there are 10,000 French citizens, including the native Jews, but the old population maintains its almost complete life undisturbed.

I had a good guide and companion about this city— a young Berber, twenty-seven years old, whose name was Muhammed Ouled Muhammed ben Makhtar. He had served five years in the French Army, and during the war was in the 6th regiment of Algerian Tirailleurs. Together we visited mosques, markets, and streets full of shops, where workers were employed making beautifully embroidered saddles, the forms, the decorations, and the trappings being precisely those still employed by certain old Mexican saddle-makers of California We saw other shops making slippers and delicate garments. Cafés emitted fragrant odors of coffee being ground and roasted. There were bakeries where loaves, each marked with the owner's name, are sent for the final stage of the oven. We entered "fonduks", or little inns, where the horses and asses are quartered in the courts below, and the visitors in rooms above, and which are the exact counterparts of the "fondas" of Spain and Spanish-America. We visited a bath or "hammam" built entirely in Moorish style. A central room with domed roof, supported by pillars and arches, led to various resting chambers, furnished with mats and pillows. By a dark corridor we reached the hot room. There were fires below; water splashed and arose in thick steam; the temperature was very high; in the dark alcoves bathers lounged and perspired.

One interesting call was upon a barber who was also a dentist. He was a grave and handsome man. Outside his shop were suspended, as evidence of his skill, scores of decayed teeth which he had extracted. He showed me his instrument—a gimlet-like tool with a point bent sideways into a strong hook. His third speciality, he told me, was the lancing of boils. Altogether he must be a most useful man to his community.

An afternoon was occupied in a long drive in a carriage driven by an old Israelite. We went out of the town through ancient cemeteries, crowded with tomb-

stones and the domed sepulchres of "marabouts," to
the village of Bou Medine. The road wound through
gardens of ancient olive trees, pomegranates, and figs.
Streams of clear water gushed down the hillsides and
along the borders of the road. Bou Medine contains
an exquisite mosque constructed in 1339. The great
doors, covered with ornamental bronze, are believed to
be Spanish work and the price paid for the ransom of
captives. There is a decayed university or *médersa* dating from the fourteenth century. Within its one time
rich interior were found only three or four young boys
who were chanting passages of the Koran, inscribed
on wooden boards.

West of Tlemcen lies another famous site—that of
the ancient city of Mansoura, the "conqueress." It was
built on a magnificent slope of the mountains, and was
completely destroyed in wars toward the end of the
fourteenth century. Only the bastions of the walls remain, and the ruins of the mosque, whose lonely tower
has been dedicated by the French government as a
"national monument." This minaret, still scintillating
with diamond-shaped bits of beautiful faience, looks
down upon a great rectangular enclosure nearly a
mile square, of whose walls only a line of fortified
towers remain. The deserted site of this once beautiful
and busy city bears to-day only straggling orchards,
and an overgrowth of prickly pears.

French influence, while scrupulously respecting native life and institutions, has, in this city of Tlemcen,
moderated the fanaticism of the Berber. The mosques
may be entered and explored. The demeanor of the

natives is friendly, courteous, and approachable. It is
a good place in which to study the results of the con-
siderate policy of attraction, which French colonial
empire pursues.

In front of the *mairie* the class of conscripts had
been called up and was being examined. All nationalities were included—French, naturalized Europeans,
natives, and Jews. There was no discrimination. All
were enrolled and subject to the same law of military
service. Pains were obviously taken to give this military summons a patriotic character. People were buy-
ing badges, formed of the French colors and the number of the class, and giving them to these young men
as they emerged from their examination, apparently
proud to be passed into service with the colors. There
were all types of the famous Algerian soldiers whose
qualities as "storm troops" were exhibited during the
World War. Amidst the fair and ruddy complexions of
the sons of European settlers, and the darker skins of
Berbers and Jews, were to be seen the features and hair
of descendants of the African race. These blacks or
mulattoes, while not numerous, are incorporated in
military units with their other fellow-citizens. I saw
the same negro types in 1920 and 1923 among the
troops stationed along the Moselle Valley and the
Rhine. Their presence in Algerian units may be the
source of the denunciations against the employment of
negro troops in German occupied territory.

From Tlemcen, the extension of the Algerian railway
carries one in a few hours to Oudjda, the eastern city
of Morocco. It was a cold night when I arrived. A dry,

chilling wind was whirling up across the steppes. The
two main hotels were filled. I found a very modest
accommodation at the "Hotel Coloniale," kept by a
stout French woman. My room was exactly that of a
Mexican inn. It was a small space entered from a patio
with no opening but the door; its floor was on a level
with the ground, but was well paved with tile. It was
clean, whitewashed, and furnished with a good bed
which took up most of the room. The auto-bus was to
leave at five o'clock the next morning for Fez, so I
bought my ticket, paid my modest hotel reckoning, and
engaged an Arab boy to call me at four. Two hours
before dawn I awoke to a dark and rainy morning, got
a cup of coffee, and sought the garage.

The motor trip from Oudjda to Fez occupied altogether about fifteen hours. The distance is 352 kilometers. For most of the distance, the route is through
a narrow plain which divides the ranges of the Atlas
and of the Riff, and which, geologists affirm, was, in
Miocene times, a strait uniting the Mediterranean
Sea with the Atlantic ocean. This is the famous "Corridor of Taza." It is the natural line of communication
between Morocco and Algeria, but, owing to the tribes
who occupy this plain, or who descend with facility
from the mountains on both sides, it presents a problem
from the military standpoint. The French did not succeed in opening communication through this passageway until 1912, and it was pacified only after 1915.
A very light military railroad has been laid through this
couloir to supply the posts which guard the passage.
Travel by automobile is more practical and far more

THE MINARET AT BOU MEDINE NEAR TLEMCEM

LOOKING OVER FEZ FROM THE ROOF OF A MEDERSA
At the left is a student engaged in prayer facing Mecca

WITHIN A MEDERSA, FEZ

rapid than by rail. The military posts are like Roman camps, each surrounded by strong loop-holed walls. Besides Taza, there are a few small towns—El Aioun, Taourirt, and El Guersif. Apart from these, one sees little of inhabited places, except the camps of the Berbers and their flocks of sheep and camels.

It was this long passageway that was threatened by the "harkas" of Abd-el-Krim in the spring and summer of 1925. The line of French posts in the foothills toward the Riff frontier could be easily penetrated by swift movements of the Riffi, and special danger lay in the disaffection of the nomadic tribes. Two of these, in the vicinity of Taza, renounced their loyalty to the French and went over to Abd-el-Krim. Taza was held, but the civil population was evacuated. It was a difficult military situation that the French faced in July, 1925, but it was handled with skill. Reinforcements were brought in from Algeria and from France. Military command was united under Marshal Pétain. The successive thrusts of Krim were repelled; the line of French outposts restored; and the Riff was penetrated. Cut off from support and from supplies, the famous Moorish leader surrendered to the French, and is now in exile on the island of Réunion.

Toward the end of the day, the road passed out from its narrow corridor, and ran among low hills where olive orchards appeared and cultivation began. Two hours after dark, the sky having cleared, the moonlight drenched the hillsides on every hand. We sped over a rise and looked down upon the gleaming lights of a great city spreading through a sloping valley. It was Fez. The car coursed along beneath ancient walls, broken by bastions and arched gates, through groves and gardens, and over a rushing stream, then dashed into the city, and stopped in the midst of a crowded and noisy square alongside the Jewish quarter or Mellah.

Amidst the clamor of boys, fighting for passengers' baggage, and the jostling of a heterogeneous crowd, no one gave any attention to anyone else's affairs. The chauffeur disappeared; the little company of passengers melted into the crowd. I put my valise on the back of a youngster, told him to take me to the Hotel Trans-Atlantique, and plunged into a labyrinth of narrow, noisy streets filled with oriental figures streaming in every direction amidst shops and bazaars. We crossed courts, passed under gateways, walked a long way. I was tired, and longed for the shelter of a quiet room. Presently the voice of a cab driver, speaking the familiar language of Spain, fell on my ear, and I gladly bundled into his rickety little equipage, and was borne away to the hotel. The end of the ride was a charming surprise—a return to European conditions set in Moorish surroundings.

I shall not attempt an adequate description of Fez. Pictures give some idea of its appearance, but they imperfectly present its life, its wonders, and its mystery. One plunges first of all into the "souk"—the quarter of shops and industry. It is a maze of narrow streets and little courts resounding with the noise of labor and traffic and full of animation. Here are practiced all the beautiful arts and handiworks of Moorish civilization. There are food shops odoriferous with spices, fruitmarkets, shops for the fabrication of rich and delicate garments, shoes, "baboush" or slippers, embroideries, carpets, silk textiles, leather work, books, book bindings, pottery-ware, brass objects, ironwork. Every need of an organized, abundant, and yet simple life is here met by things that are desirable, serviceable, and elegant, and that display human handicraft in admirable and artistic designs. I felt as a Christian crusader must have felt on coming from a rude and barren life into the rich and beautiful culture of the Orient. In fact, the sights before my eyes, the very types of people, their garments, their behavior, were exactly what the warriors of Europe viewed with amazement in the East eight hundred years ago, and, beholding, turned from conquest to trade.

The streets and shops in their narrow proportions, their busy activity, their streaming throngs, recall those of Canton or Peking; but there is a difference—an immense difference. These streets and their people were clean; their garments were choicer than those of any European people; not a single bad odor assailed the senses, but only the aromatic scents of the East and the fresh perfumes of cedar and sandalwood. On all sides, currents of pure water gurgled and splashed. Fountains and bathing places abounded, for these are essential for the ablutions that must precede prayer. Such a fountain is shown in the illustration facing page 65. Below a beautifully tiled facade is an ample trough or basin into which clear water constantly splashes. In the rear is a "house of merchandise" in

which wholesale merchants display samples and wares.
The interior is as artistic as the outside. Three stories
rise around a patio. Walls, ceilings and doorways are
perfect examples of carving and ornamentation.

The predominant types were Caucasian—tall, splendid figures, soft wavy hair and beards, frequently light
brown or blond, eyes that were sometimes blue, noses
long, straight, and only rarely aquiline. On all sides,
doors opened into the serenity of shrines and mosques
where men, at all hours, the cares of life abandoned,
were prostrating themselves before God. An atmosphere
of religious mystery, impenetrable, almost repellant,
fills the city of Fez. Little donkeys and mules crowd
through the streets laden with bulky panniers or bearing proud riders seated on richly ornamented saddles.
Women were numerous too, but except for an occasional Jewess or a group of mountain Berbers, they
were wrapped closely in white cloaks and veiled up to
the eyes.

For hours I passed and wandered, lost to all sense
of orientation, and each moment surprised anew by
fresh beauty of gateway, or façade, or by the rich
materials in shops and bazaars. Then, to get a sense of
direction, and to locate this amazing place, I was
guided to the north side of the city through the Bab
Guissa and on to the hills, where lie the ancient tombs
and cemeteries of Fez. The panorama was magnificent.
The city extends for nearly four miles through its sloping valley. It is surrounded with ancient ramparts.
Above the flat roofs and higher dwellings spring the
great minarets. Across the valley and at the foot of the

city are thick greeneries of gardens and orchards; far away rise ranges of mountains, white with a recent fall of snow. I followed up the hills southward to the walls of "New Fez"—Fez Djedid. It was Thursday, on which day, outside the wall, a stock market assembles. There were troops of little donkeys tethered by a forefoot to picket lines. There were horses, mules, camels, goats, and sheep. It was a scene of violent chaffering.

A call upon the French authorities of the city procured passes for visits to the museums and the three "médersas" or universities. These latter buildings are among the most beautiful pieces of architecture of Fez. All the glory of interior decoration and plaster chiseling of which one sees remnants in Spain, may here be examined in completeness. These médersas do not correspond to a European type of school. They are not equipped with classrooms, for the instruction takes place at the adjacent mosques or under their walls. The médersa is a dwelling house for the students—a kind of glorified fraternity house—where the long-robed, dignified students of Arabic religion and law make their homes.

As I experienced the overpowering sensations imposed by the city of Fez, I could but contrast it with the city of Rome, which I had left but a few days before. Here within a few hours travel of one another, Rome and Fez embody the contrasts of western and oriental civilizations—civilizations that for a thousand years have contended with one another—the conflict of the Crescent and the Cross. One's wonder is renewed, not that Christian Europe has come to prevail, but that such a city and civilization as Fez could maintain itself independent and unconquered.down to the present day, so close to Europe's coast and frontiers.

From Fez one may travel westward to Meknes and the Atlantic Coast by a railroad which has a branch under construction headed for Tangier. The accommodations, time schedules, and charges are satisfactory, though the automobile is much used. At Meknes the French have taken pains, as they have elsewhere, to establish the foreign quarter and municipal organization outside the ancient city, leaving the latter, protected by its conservatism, to maintain the old life facing the new. This was wise policy on the part of Marshal Lyautey, and the plan of developing the new towns is splendidly conceived. The work of laying out these French suburbs was entrusted to a specialist, M. Prost, who designed the extension of the city of Antwerp. It has been accomplished with foresight, wisdom, and imagination.

The view one has of Meknes from the new town is across a little valley or gorge filled with green trees and gardens. The city lies on a ridge, and presents a skyline of walls, gates, and magnificent towers. Outside of the city are the extensive palaces, mosques, and gardens of former sultans. Here the great emperor of the seventeenth century, Moulay Ismaïl, made his capital and gave to Meknes a temporary glory. He is said to have maintained an army of fifteen thousand blacks, brought across the desert from the valleys of the Senegal and Niger. Their descendants are visible on the streets today. The palace grounds embrace the imperial residence, drill-fields, gardens, and stables, and are enclosed in a rampart with a circumference that must be more than a mile. The stables are curious, and cover many acres. The roofs have gone, but there remain the walls and hundreds of arches and columns between which were the paddocks of highly pedigreed animals. Arab historians assert that these stables once sheltered twelve thousand horses and mules. In a part of these grounds lives Moulay el Hassan, the deposed descendant of the great Ismaïl.

As in all Moorish cities, there is a mellah or Jewish ghetto. Israelites appear to be a very ancient class in Morocco, originating in Punic and Roman times, but their numbers were greatly increased by the expulsions from Spain. They were allowed to have, in each city, their own magistrates, their council where they settled their private affairs, their synagogues and their schools; but they were subject to humiliations and oppressions, and were confined to their own quarter of the town. I visited the mellah of Meknes on a Saturday. The shops were closed. The men and women and children were on the streets in holiday attire. The costumes of the Jewish women were gay. Their headdresses reminded one of the women of Andalucía. Many of the young girls were handsome—with the comeliness of daughters of Israel. The Jewish men wore the long black gowns and round caps, the habit of their race in many lands.

Meknes is an important military center for the French. It has been the base for the columns penetrating and conquering the Atlas Mountains to the southward. Meknes is also the center of Mohammedan fanaticism—the headquarters of the sect of snake charmers and fanatical devotees, called the Aïssawa. Here, as at Marrakech, further south, the squares of the native city are filled all day long with crowds watching wild half-naked men of the desert charm venomous reptiles. The snakes are three: the tiny asp, the puffed adder, about the length of a big rattle snake, but much heavier of body, and the black cobra. One is assured by good authority that the fangs and poison sacs of these serpents have not been removed.

For the headquarters of their protectorate over Morocco, the French have selected the city of Rabat, and, back of the old Moorish city, they have begun the building of a splendidly planned modern town. The buildings that are rising here for the accommodation of the bureaus and offices of the protectorate are not only very fine and solid in construction, but they have the great merit of being patterned on the lines of Moorish architecture. Modern in their conveniences, they are splendidly native in appearance and composition. They evidence by their solidity of construction the permanence of French rule, and at the same time, by their harmony with the finest achievements of Moorish architecture, they indicate the disposition to preserve and support the best of the ancient civilization.

A considerable river—the Bou Regreg—reaches the

Atlantic at this point. The harbors of Morocco are
open and inadequate. In this case, a low bluff on the
south protects the mouth of the river, forming a broad
estuary or haven, which, in spite of the bar, can be
entered by small vessels. It was such shelter which gave
to this point of Morocco its evil history as a corsairs'
lair. On the south side of the harbor is the Moorish
city of Rabat, while on the north is Salee. The pirates
of Salee have a large place in the history of.European
commerce, and are immortalized in the pages of one
of the greatest examples of English fiction, Defoe's
"Robinson Crusoe." Crusoe, it will be recalled, was
taken prisoner by the corsairs, and carried to Salee,
where he remained for some time the slave of a Moorish master. He finally escaped on the counterpart of
one of the feluccas, which, with pointed sails set high,
still slip in and out of the harbor of Salee throughout
the hours of the day. In Rabat the old médersa which
stands on the bluff above the river has been charmingly
re-arranged as a museum, and here may be seen examples of the heavy chains that one time hung on the
necks and limbs of the European captives, brought to
this mart for disposition.

Salee was, in the early centuries of the Christian
era, a Roman town, and perhaps the southernmost post
of Roman arms on the Atlantic coast. Adjacent to
Rabat, lie the ruins of Chella, from which have been
recovered Roman inscriptions, and about whose Moorish remains there is an atmosphere of mystery and
charm. Above the adjacent plain, towers a structure of

great beauty—the tower of Hassan—the minaret of an
abandoned and ruined mosque widely famous in its
day.

Rabat has interest as being the rendezvous of the
troops assembled for the conquest of Spain. In the seventh and eighth centuries, it appears to have been a
great "Arab" camp. The Arab element was probably
small, the mere general staff of the forces drawn here
for the invasion of Europe, but the prospect of rich
pillage drew after these Arab leaders the indigenous
population of Tunisia, Algeria, and Morocco, forming
the forces led by Tarik and those who followed after
him to the conquest of Córdoba and the peninsula.

Marshal Lyautey was not at Rabat during my visit
to that city, having been called to France by the necessity of a surgical operation, but I was very kindly
received at the offices of the Protectorate by the Delegate, M. Blanc. In a conversation which exhibited wide
historical and ethnological knowledge, M. Blanc emphasized the separateness of the Berbers from the
world of orthodox Mohammedanism, their relatively
late conversion, their rejection of the Koranic law and
of the kadis, their essentially democratic organization
and their adherence to their own agglutinative Berber
language. These facts may simplify the problem of
French administration. The Arab language, law and
prejudices do not have to be regarded. The Berbers
may be introduced directly to the language and culture
of France. The schools which will be established among
the interior tribes will not be based upon Arab language
and literature, but upon French. It was obvious that

this administrator felt great hopes for these Berber
peoples and for the future of French influence among
them. He stated that while the military conquest of
the Atlas had been difficult, it was nearing completion. At that date no tribe, which had once submitted
to French authority, had ever revolted. Here, he believed, was a people virile, resourceful, intelligent, and
capable of responding to new moral appeals.

Through the kindness of M. Blanc I had a very interesting meeting with a group of French scholars at
Rabat, to whom have been committed the tasks of
organizing instruction, of preserving the fine arts and
handicrafts of Morocco, of advancing the linguistic and
ethnological knowledge of the land. The spirit under-
lying these efforts is to preserve the best of the race
and of its culture, to make education practical, and
French science and culture the instruments for the
wise development of Berber civilization. One of these
gentlemen, it may be remarked, had adopted the Mohammedan faith, and wore the characteristic garments
of a Mohammedan scholar. The scientific study of the
country and its peoples, which is so marked a character
of the French policy, has found its appropriate, schol-
arly organization in the *Institut des Hautes-Études
Marocaines*, which is located at Rabat. It holds scientific conferences, and publishes an admirable bulletin,
entitled *Hespéris*, the publication of which was commenced in 1921.

The most important European center in Morocco is
not Rabat, the capital, but Casablanca, further south
on the Atlantic coast. The common name for this

city is simply the Spanish translation of the Arabic name—*Dar el Beïda*—the "White House." Outside of Tangier, this has long been the principal point of European entrance into the country, and it was here, to stop riot and massacre, that the French began their military conquest of the country in 1907.

This place was chosen by Marshal Lyautey as the principal port of the country, and an ambitious plan of harbor improvement was undertaken. Two great breakwaters, built out from opposite sides of the harbor, oppose themselves to the violence of the Atlantic, and create a large inner basin adequate for the shelter of shipping for a long time to come. Modern piers and shipping facilities have been erected, and the traffic of the port has grown to considerable proportions. The modern city is extensive. It is laid out according to scientific ideas of city planning, with broad avenues and circling boulevards, parks, recreation fields, military drill-grounds, and a great aviation port. A daily air service is maintained between Casablanca and Toulouse in France. There are two air stops after leaving Morocco, one in southern Spain near Madeira and the other toward the Pyrenees. During the long summer days, the flight may be made in a single day. Both passengers and air mail are regularly carried.

The growth of the city of Casablanca, since French enterprise took it in hand, has been surprisingly rapid, and has probably proceeded faster than economic conditions fully justify. It must be recalled, however, by those who criticize the policy that has invested so heavily in this city and elsewhere in Morocco, that a deliberate and successful part of Marshal Lyautey's plan of holding the country during the World War was to push economic development, create a large demand for labor, and impress the native by the rapid development of markets and commercial facilities. The money spent for these things represents money saved by the reduction of the military establishment in Morocco in 1914, and the devotion of funds, that might otherwise have been employed in military operations, to the building up of serviceable constructions of ordinary life.

It is the towns of Morocco that give the land its chief interest to the traveler, and this will continue to be the case until the Atlas Mountains are sufficiently pacified to enable visitors to penetrate their recesses, camp amidst their great groves of cedar, and scale their snowy summits; and until the south Atlas region can also be opened to foreign travel, and its oases and interesting populations are approachable. These great towns have, each one of them, a separate history and a distinct character. They are the part of the population which has been most prompt to accept and support French authority. They represent the furtherest progress that the new government has made in introducing new types of administration. There are, in fact, fifteen of these great towns or "villes" in which the government of the French protectorate has created a municipal organization. They are Azemmour, Casablanca, Fez, Kenitra, Marrakech, Mazagan, Meknes, Mogador, Oudjda, Rabat, Safi, Salee, Sefrou, Settat, and Taza. The native governor or "pasha" at the head of each of these towns represents the authority of the Sultan and he reports to the grand vizier as do the "kaids" at the head of the tribes. The governors have powers both of public administration and of justice, but French authority is represented at the side of each by a chief of municipal services, who reports through the Commandant of the Region to the Direction of Civil Affairs. This French "city manager" controls the native branches of administration, and, at the same time, by a formal delegation of power from the pasha, he has the direction of certain services that have a French personnel, and which include public works, hygiene and public health, municipal finance, and police.

A first step toward representation of the population in their municipal government has been taken by the creation of municipal commissions which are consultative to the pasha and the French chief of municipal services, and are made up of the different elements of the population of the town—Europeans, Mohammedans, and Israelites. Each town has its own budget distinct from that of the Chérifien State, the receipts coming from an urban tax, market taxes, duties paid at the gates of the city, and a rather extensive series of charges made for public services. City expenses include the personnel of the municipal administration, improvement of streets and public works, slaughterhouses, maintenance of the gates and markets, municipal police, prisons, public hygiene and infirmaries, etc. The largest municipal budget is that of Casablanca, which in 1920 had receipts, 9,647,000 francs, and expenses, 7,532,000 francs. The official statistics of these municipal budgets show all of these towns to be in a satisfactory, self-sustaining condition. Several made subscriptions to the bonds of the French Republic during the World War. Their life is orderly and animated. There is little evidence of destitution. There is little mendicancy, although one of the characteristic sights of the streets of these cities is the appearance at the doors of the homes of the wealthy of an occasional solicitor of alms, who by long and repeated prayers, and appeals to the mercy of a piteous God, contrives to secure a contribution that is probably traditional between the family and the dependant.

In speaking of Fez, I have already emphasized the cleanliness of these city streets and of the crowds which pour through them, but one sight disturbs the attention, particularly in Marrakech, and that is frightful evidence of venereal disease. The Berber is probably not a healthy race, and his conquests and promiscuities have spread the infections of old and loathsome complaints through a large part of Africa.

CHAPTER III

THE kingdom of Morocco is now a protectorate of European powers, but the responsibility is unequally divided. The diminished territory of the ancient "Empire of the Farthest West" (*el Maghreb el Aksa*) has been divided by foreign intervention into three distinct zones. The first is Tangier, which comprises the town of that name, facing Spain across the Straits of Gibraltar, and a small area of the peninsula, providing the environs of the town. Tangier was for centuries the place of approach, the only possible entrance to the country, and, until recently, the diplomatic and consular representatives of foreign countries were stationed at this city conducting their relations with the Makhzen or Moorish government, through a minister or khalifa of the sultan.

Tangier has an international status. Its government is controlled by the consuls of the foreign powers accredited to Morocco. It does not seem to be a satisfactory government, and during 1923 diplomatic discussions took place between France, Great Britain, Italy, and Spain, the object of which appears to have been to secure a more direct responsibility for this little territory. In August, 1926, the Spanish government reopened this discussion with a request that Tangier be

48

GATEWAY TO THE CITY OF FEZ

THE GATE AT BOU JELOUD, FEZ

added to the Spanish zone. All four of these countries view this tiny African peninsula with an interest, and with a strong prejudice against its becoming exclusively the dependency of one of their number. England cannot contemplate its falling into the hands of a strong military power, like France. She would never brook a fortification here that would impair the unique power of Gibraltar. Spain has dissipated armed forces for hundreds of years on this shore of Africa, and naturally regards the assertions of interest by other nations as inferior to her own. Also, Spain finds the present status of Tangier an obstacle to her pacification of the zone of Northern Morocco over which she holds the protectorate.

The rugged Mediterranean coast of Morocco where cliffs and sterile mountains come down quite to the sea, and are only occasionally interrupted by the openings of valleys or stretches of beach, has been a field of Spanish effort since the times of Charles V. On small defensible peninsulas and islets along the coast are the Spanish "presidios," both fortified garrisons and prisons—Ceuta, Peñon de Velez, Alhucemas, Melilla, and a group of barren islets—las Chafarinas.

A few miles from the coast, on the east side of the peninsula of Tangiers, is the city of Tetuan, founded in 1492 by Moorish and Jewish exiles from Spain. This city was captured in 1860 by a Spanish army under General O'Donnell. Conquest was renewed and a few years later by another Spanish force under General Prim. Spanish arms have won scant glory since the peninsula wars of Napoleon, and it is quite interesting to note the luster that attends these minor operations around Tetuan. O'Donnell and Prim both became prime ministers of Spain. Their victories have been celebrated in Spanish music and story. Years ago, traveling on the Island of Panay in the Philippines, I came on a village church, well built of stone, constructed by some Spanish friar-missionary in the latter half of the 19th century, the entire façade of which, above the doors, was decorated by a triumphal representation in bas-relief of the capture of Tetuan.

The peninsula of Melilla has been held by the Spaniards since 1497, and it is mainly from this port that Spanish efforts to penetrate and conquer the Riff mountains have been made in recent years. But the difficult ranges of the Riff mountains and their defiant Berber inhabitants have defeated this inland penetration. It was the retirement of the Spanish lines from advanced positions south of Melilla that encouraged the Riff leader, Abd-el-Krim, in the spring of 1925, to undertake his venturesome assaults upon the French lines on the southern foothills of this mountain range.

The line of demarcation between Spanish and French zones has never been surveyed or exactly laid down, due to the fact that neither of these countries has ever successfully attempted to carry its lines of outposts to their joint frontier, but, in general, the delimitation begins on the Atlantic coast some miles south of Larache, and runs easterly to the valley of the Lukkus River just south of the city of El Kzar-el Kbir. It then follows the river valley into the mountains that separate the two holy cities of Sheshuan (Spanish zone) and Ouezzane (French zone). It then meanders along the crest of the Riff mountains until it reaches the Moulouya river, whence it follows the left bank of this stream to the Mediterranean. All the rest of Morocco constitutes the French protectorate except a small Spanish possession on the south coast, called Ifni.

The natural feature which dominates this part of Africa, and gives it its character, is the range of Atlas Mountains, which, in a northeasterly and southwesterly direction, separate the northwestern end of the continent from the interior. The Middle Atlas embraces the central and northerly mass of the range; the Great Atlas is the southwesterly portion, while the Little Atlas is a distinct range south of the Great Atlas, and divided from it by the populous valley of the Sous. This imposing chain of mountains rises 2,000 feet higher than the California Sierras, and is capped by perpetual snows. They are the source of the streams that reach the Atlantic to the north and the west, and on the southern slopes form the dry fossil courses called "oueds" or "wadis," and give rise to the desert oases. The slopes of these mountains are forested by cedar, oak, and conifers. The valleys and elevated plateaus are the homes of the sedentary Berber tribes, the pure and indigenous population of North Africa—tribes that remained unconquered through successive centuries of history, but which, with minor exceptions, have today made their submission to French authority.

The manner in which the French have secured the

submission of these Berbers is striking. It has been a combination of diplomacy and military force, but diplomacy has achieved most. The military arm has been a reserve, held in the background, used only occasionally, and then as a last resort, in quick hard blows, to break an opposition that solicitation can not overcome. Nowhere has the French policy of penetration been pursued with more remarkable results, and with so great an exhibition of patience, skill, and understanding. It is a policy associated with the name of Marshal Lyautey, but developed by him as a result of long experience with the comparable problems presented by the populations of Madagascar and Algeria.

The instrument for the pacific subjugation of the Berbers in Morocco is a corps of intelligence officers called the *Service des Renseignements.* I suppose there may be 200 officers in this service—carefully selected young men of talent and devotion. They are masters of both the Arabic and Berber tongues. They are students of Mohammedan religion and law, and of the Berber institutions, which it is their duty to understand and to protect. These officers have pushed out beyond the line of French posts and established their work in contact with the "unsubmitted tribes." There they study the conditions confronting French authority, win the friendship of Berber leaders, detect and analyze the growth of local hostility, and pursue by arts of persuasion a policy of convincing the Berbers of the advantages of French rule.

Only as a last resort is a military demonstration called for. Then a little expedition of a few thousand men is quickly mobilized and the blow follows; but even during the process of hostilities, and this is quite in accord with the customs of the Berbers themselves, negotiation proceeds and fighting stops the moment that conciliation has a chance to win. This seems to have been the method employed by Lyautey, and at no time with greater success than during the World War, when the armed forces in Morocco were reduced to the slenderest proportions. The military columns that compose these expeditions into the Atlas seem to be normally composed of several distinct elements. First there is a battalion of Moroccan infantry, Berbers trained by France to conquer Berbers. These soldiers, both in Africa and France, have won encomiums for their fighting qualities, but they are undoubtedly difficult to handle. The quarrelsome, thieving, deceptive, traits of the North African Mohammedans display themselves among these troops, and are only repressed by the firm character of French discipline and the remarkable qualities of the French officer personnel. Brigaded with such a Moroccan detachment, is invariably a battalion of blacks, rifle-men of the Senegal and the Sudan, docile, dependable, and capable of prodigious endurance. But a third element is necessary— a force unshakable by any of the sources of demoralization to be found in an African army, a force hardened to any adventure, a force of white soldiers. These soldiers are white, but they are not Frenchmen. French authority is jealous of the spilling of French blood. The nation has been "bled white" far beyond any anticipations of Bismarck's rough phrase. French lives are precious; the question of population is too dubious to permit Frenchmen to be lost in colonial campaigns. For these reasons, and in obedience to a most logical and cold-blooded "economy of military forces," the French employ, for the stiffening of their military expeditions, a battalion of expatriated white men—the Foreign Legion.

Before the World War this famous corps embraced only two regiments—one serving in Africa, and one in Asia. It was composed largely of mature men of broken lives—men who either by reason of crushing poverty, or, not infrequently, by reason of shame, were compelled to dis-sever the relations of home and country and obliterate themselves in a fighting force, in which no personal questions were ever asked. This old Foreign Legion, used by the French since the beginning of African conquests in the thirties, disappeared in the World War. It was renewed again and again, only to melt away in the furious shock attacks in which it was used. Since the World War, the Foreign Legion has been raised to the strength of a division. The conditions of service remain as before. The remuneration is the scantiest, the discipline the severest, the life the most onerous and dangerous of perhaps any troops in the world. Yet, in spite of these conditions, the Foreign Legion maintains its old reputation and morale.

As I saw these men in North Africa, they appeared to be young—not different in appearance or behavior from the lads who make' up any modern army. They had just returned from the Atlas campaign of 1923, and were settling in their quarters at their principal posts for a period of repose. Some of them were Russian, some British; four of them in the Moroccan force, I was informed, were Americans; but the majority, five years after the end of the World War, were what the bulk of the Foreign Legion has always been—men of German birth.

The total armed strength of the French establishment in Morocco before the critical conditions of 1925, was about 60,000 men—Berbers, blacks, Foreign Legion, French Artillery, and French Flying Service. To defeat Abd-el-Krim, it was necessary to bring in the XIX Corps from Algeria, and one division from France, together with a large amount of special artillery and flying units. The normal garrison is distributed in small detachments along the Riff foothills and the slopes of the Atlas, each post fortified and organized, as were posts of the Roman legions two thousand years ago, connected by an excellent system of communications and supported by reserves based on Meknes and Casablanca. Beyond the line of such posts, negotiation and administration are in the hands of officers of the Intelligence Service.

Foreign rights in Morocco rest upon a number of treaties of which the most important are the Convention of Madrid of 1880 and the General Act of the Algeciras Conference of 1906, to both of which treaties the United States was a party. The Treaty of Protection, which placed the government of Morocco, outside of Tangier and the Spanish zone, under French control, was dated March 30, 1912. By the first two treaties, equality of economic opportunity in Morocco was assured to the signers and this equality, except for some minor conditions, continues to protect the common trading and commercial interests of foreign nations. These treaties also gave, to the foreign nations signing them, extra-territoriality—the right to immunity for their citizens or subjects from Moroccan police and judicial administration; the right, in other words, of persons of foreign nationality to trial in consular courts of their own states. A similar jurisdiction was extended by these treaties over the entire personnel of the consulates, including their military guards, and also over native agents and employees in limited numbers of foreign firms doing business in the country. To be one of these *protégés* of a foreign nation is a coveted privilege to a Moorish merchant.

The French government, as it has modernized the administration of courts and police and strengthened its position in the country, has sought to secure a surrender of these so-called "Capitulations" by her former co-signers of the Moroccan treaties. She has succeeded in all cases but two—Great Britain and the United States. Spain, Italy, and Belgium voluntarily cancelled their extra-territorial rights. Germany and Austria were forced to surrender their status in Morocco by the Treaties of Versailles and Saint Germain. But the English and American governments attach importance to the principle of extra-territoriality in Morocco, and remain obdurate to French suggestions. Thus, technically, the American in Morocco is not subject to the courts of the country, but only to the authority of his own consul.

Am I not myself conscious of these privileges? Was I not arrested for having improperly gone over the side of a vessel before she had docked, and then was I not promptly discharged by the *commissaire de police,* while my partner in offense, a foreigner of another nationality, was held for examination? Did I not, on my daily visits to the American consulate, receive the salutes of two Moorish "soldiers" posted at the consul's door, where they served the flag of the United States in their own remote country? And was I not banqueted by a Moor, the wealthy Taibi ben Hadj Thamy Hadáwei, who is a protégé of the United States of America? This banquet was arranged for me by the American consul—a cultivated gentleman, and a graduate of Harvard University, to whom the foreign service of the United States is a profession. He had served some years in Sicily, and then in Morocco, and has now been advanced to an important consulate in South America. The third guest was a gentleman of Spanish descent, a native of Tangier. We reached the house of Taibi, the son of the pilgrim Thamy Hadáwei, by a narrow and unprepossessing thoroughfare. The gloom of the night was unrelieved by street illumination. The front of the house was plain, and of a sort not likely to attract the attention of a tax gatherer. The entrance to a Moorish house accords with the social prejudices of the country. One is admitted through the outer portal into a passageway that proceeds straight ahead for a few paces, then turns sharply to the right, then again to the left until it reaches the interior court of the dwelling. The object of this traverse is to protect the women of the household, from the sight of passers-by.

We were met by our host and conducted to an upper chamber furnished with innumerable rugs of beauty and value. Our seats were low circular leather cushions, which assist one in sitting comfortably, cross-legged on the floor. Brass lavers and napkins were brought in for the customary ablutions. Then a little low table a few feet in diameter was placed in the center between the four of us. The Moors, in the course of developing an elaborate and luxurious civilization, have devised a really delicious and bountiful cuisine. A good appetite is for the Moors a matter of national pride, not to say national honor. The dining habits are simple. There are no separate dishes, no forks, no spoons, no knives. The hand takes the place of them all, but only the right hand. The preliminary skirmish of conversation was not prolonged, and very soon the banquet began to arrive.

Now, I have observed, as the result of travels in all the continents, that the memories that gleam brightest in the mind are those connected with satisfactory food, and that nothing so cheers a discourse before a general audience as a description of foreign viands and their service. Wherefore I kept careful notes of this simple dinner, and I am prepared to tell all about it.

The first thing that was placed on our little table was an enormous pie called "bastila," obviously a corruption of the Spanish·word "pastel." It was cooked in a very deep pan; it measured quite two feet in diameter. The crust was highly shortened and covered over with powdered sugar and cinnamon. It was stuffed with pigeon giblets. The opening phase of the engagement consisted of a right-handed assault by each of us upon his respective quarter of this pie. It was a good pie, and we did not cease our attentions to it for some time. This was then removed, and there was brought in a roasted lamb, which is the *chef d'œuvre* of every Moorish banquet. This mutton had been roasted with butter and an oil called "argan." This oil is peculiarly a product of Morocco, and is derived from the kernel of the fruit of a tree which grows for a short distance along the coast around Mogador, and nowhere else in the world. This grove is the last stand of a vanishing tropical forestation. Foreigners object to argan oil, and it does have the quality of rapidly turning "high," but when fresh it not only gives tenderness and savor to a roast, but browns the exterior into a delicious flaky "crackle." Again, with the bare right hand we assailed course number two. The meat was so tender that there was no difficulty in separating the portions desired, and our host, in obedience to the exacting code of Moorish hospitality, insisted on prying loose, with his fingers, various choice morsels and supplying them to his guests.

After we had disposed of the sheep, there came in course number three. This consisted of roasted capons, large and magnificent fowls, cooked with butter and olives. To be sure, there were only three of these for four men, but to make up for any seeming deficiency, these big, fattened chickens were blanketed over by an enormous "tortilla" or omelet of beaten eggs and chopped giblets, olives, and seasoning.

Following this course, there appeared an enormous platter of meat balls called *kĕfta*. These were made of beef cooked with allspice and other condiments, and banked about with lentils, greens, tomatoes, and onions. I am afraid that by this time our enthusiasm had begun to decline, and that we failed to do justice to this magnificent production. But, happily, the brother of our host appeared at the right moment—a very valiant trencherman, whom the Spaniard said he himself had seen eat a whole sheep alone—and this ready ally cleared up the platter of beef balls.

Then came a second magnificent pie of the same depth, proportions, and general character as the first, but this one was stuffed with a delicious confection of almond paste, called *m'hanghah*. Well, we ate what we could of this pie. After this there were served fruits. Morocco is the home of splendid fruits; and there were also delicious bananas from the Canary Islands.

This course was followed by an elaborate ceremony of tea drinking. The Moor is very fond of tea, and he makes good tea, although he sweetens it excessively with chunks of sugar broken from large crystallized cones. To the tea he adds large quantities of fresh mint. This mint-tea concoction he regards as an essential for the completion of every feast, and its need I am not prepared to dispute. The tea was prepared and served by the host himself, and formed the completion of our modest repast.

One other fact I feel compelled to add. There was wine served with this banquet, and our host partook as well as his guests. It may be asked, how, in a society from which alcoholic beverages were banned by the injunction of the Prophet, may a gentleman of good standing in his church, himself the son of a pilgrim, serve and partake of wine? Well, the answer seems to be that the Moors, like the members of other refined societies, have their lawyers to help them out of legal difficulties. There is one passage of the Koran in which Mohammed says: "One *single drop* of wine is accursed." The Moorish practice is to fill the goblet, dip the end of a finger until a single drop adheres, then shake this drop off on the ground and curse it. The rest can then be consumed within the precepts of religion.

I have referred to our American consul in Morocco, our sole representative in that country, who placed me under many obligations by his kindness. I gathered from him that the job would be a very fine one if there were no Americans in Morocco. But unfortunately, for the consulate, there is one American family, resident and claiming rights in the land. It happened in this way. Many years ago a Moor, for reasons that are not disclosed, migrated to America and took up his abode in the city of New Orleans. Here he married, the bride being a lady who had come to the United States from the Kingdom of Italy. Three sons and three daughters were the happy issue of this union, all American-born citizens of Mediterranean derivation, and all speaking the English language with the soft southern drawl of

Louisiana creoles. The father and mother both died. The father, in his familiar accounts of his native land, had implanted in the children the firm conviction that they were the heirs to Moroccan estates embracing a considerable portion of the ancient sultanate. They decided to return to the land of their fathers and claim their heritage. They have done so, and have managed to discover large and promising possessions, which they implore the American consul to bestir himself and legally place in their hands. One eloquent letter was particularly concerned with property near Mogador where, as their epistle touchingly reads: "Grandfather lies buried in the sands."

But outside of the exacting appeals of this small American colony in Morocco, the task of the American consul seems to be largely to watch over and affirm the treaty rights of the United States of America in that dominion, and to frame designs for a participation in its commerce by our too casual American business men. The United States takes a large part of one of the most interesting exports of Morocco, namely, goat skins, which, beautifully tanned and dyed, go mainly to Philadelphia, and are known to the trade as Morocco leather. In return we export to Morocco a few things in which our foreign trade is everywhere distinguished, namely: automobiles, Singer sewing machines (although these are probably made at Scotch factories), and petroleum and its derivatives. The harbor at which American oil enters Morocco is the new port of Fedala, where tank installations have been erected.

British trade furnishes much of the tea, which is

green China, but into this trade French exporters are now cutting. The British also furnish candles, a commerce in which the Italians compete; but most of all, the British furnish cotton goods, wherein the manufactures of Lancashire are supreme. The French supply silk and most of the sugar, which must be sent in large granulated cones. American manufacturers could undoubtedly participate in this sugar trade did they not refuse to supply it in cones. Altogether, the foreign trade of Morocco is a growing one. In 1920 imports amounted to over 1,000,000,000 francs, of which France and Algeria contributed nearly 65%. The United States furnished imports, to the value of francs, 40,000,000. The exports from the French zone of Morocco are less than a third of the imports, and amounted in 1920 to not quite 300,000,000 francs. (*Protectorat Français au Maroc: Annuaire Économique et Financier*, 1921-1922).

Organizing the government of the Protectorate, the French have taken pains to leave the sultan in a position of dignity and nominal power. He is the legal sovereign of the country. All acts are done in his name. All legislation takes the form of imperial decrees or *dahirs*. But the actual government is vested in the High Commissioner of the French Republic. The decree of the President of the French Republic of June 11, 1912, provides that the representative of the French Republic shall have the title of *Commissaire Résident Général*, reporting to the Minister of Foreign Affairs. He is the "depository of all the powers of the French Republic in the Chérifien Empire"; he is the sole inter-

mediary of the sultanate with representatives of foreign
powers; he approves and promulgates the decrees of
"His Chérifien Majesty"; he is commander-in-chief of
the land forces, and has the disposition of the naval
forces. He is assisted by a Delegate to the Residency
General, who, in his absence, takes his place.

The government of Morocco, before the French intervention, followed a traditional form. The sultan was
not only politically an autocrat; he was "Khalif,
Chief of Islam, Commander of the Faithful," at once
a temporal and a spiritual ruler. The succession of a
sultan to his high position required the acceptance of
the Oulema or learned council of Fez, but once on the
throne, he was as absolute as an autocrat may be. He
was assisted by five ministers or "viziers"—a grand
vizier, a minister of foreign affairs, who at times resided
at Tangiers, a minister of war, a minister of finance,
and a minister of "reclamations," who dealt with the
complaints and affairs of the tribes. The French protectorate has suppressed all but one of these ancient
vizierates, namely, the office of grand vizier, but has
added three new ones held by Moors; a ministry of
justice, which includes also worship, a ministry of the
domains, and a ministry of the "habous." These habous
are pious foundations or trusts created by the devout
for the support of Mohammedan worship and instruction.

Under these ministries, which with the sultanate
form the Maghzen of Chérifien State, there were
"kaids" or great chieftains at the head of the Berber
and Arab tribes. Over the towns were appointed

STOCK MARKET OUTSIDE THE WALLS OF FEZ

THE WALLS OF FEZ

FOUNTAIN AND HOUSE OF MERCHANDISE IN FEZ

"pashas" or governors, and throughout the cities justice was administered by "kadis."

It is obvious that under the terms of the treaty of protection and the decree of the French President, the direction of the services of foreign affairs and of war could only be performed by the Résident Général, or his assistants. In order to meet the foreign obligations of the empire, as well as to organize and develop the finances of the country, public revenue and its expenditure had likewise to be put under a French staffed department—the *Direction Générale des Finances*. There have also been organized "general directions" of public works, of colonization, of public instruction, fine arts and antiquities, and the services of public health and hygiene. The Direction of Intelligence and Native Affairs, the work of whose officers has already been mentioned, and which involves the obedience of tribes that were never fully submissive to the sultanate or to any other authority, is another task which the French have made exclusively their own. There are also offices of posts, telegraphs, and telephones, of civil and military transport, and of railways.

The government of the towns has already been described. Outside of these, the administration of Morocco is divided first into "zones"—the "zone of the front," the "zone of the rear of the front," which are under military administration, and third, the "zone of the interior" which has been completely pacified, where security is considered complete and where a civil administration has taken the place of a military. These zones are divided into "regions," at the head of which is a commandant, either civil or military, who is the delegate of the Résident Général. These regions are further divided into "cercles." The regions under civil authority are those of Oudjda, the Gharb, Rabat, Casablanca, and the "civil circumscriptions" of Mazagan, Safi, and Mogador. The regions under military authority are Taza, Fez, Meknes, and Marrakech. This description is, however, not quite complete. It does not include certain districts of the middle Atlas attached to the military regions, and it does not include Morocco south of the Grand Atlas which has a special régime. This last region comprising the valley of the Sous with its port of Agadir is at present closed to foreign commerce and to foreign visitors. It is a region inhabited by strong and restless tribes, which have never made a complete submission, which do not welcome foreign intercourse, and into which the French have never sent their military columns. The method of French control in this part of Morocco follows Roman precedents. They are endeavoring to win over this territory through the support and attachment of three great chieftains who are described as *les Grands Kaïds*. These powerful tribal heads recognize French authority and accept the responsibilities of their position. They are supported by the French in the exercise of their powers. Contacts are established entirely through officers of the *Service des Renseignements*. The rule of these Kaïds is not considered to be entirely satisfactory, for it perpetuates the old feudal system of Morocco with its abuses, severities, and tyrannical exercise of authority. But the problem is a large one, and the

French approach it cautiously. It is a situation which American authority, similarly situated, would clear up impulsively, and by hard fighting, at any cost. It resembles somewhat the old situation on Lake Lanao, which Pershing subdued by hard blows in 1903. But the French avoid violent issues. They are ready to take time, to win slowly, and they have immense confidence in their powers of persuasion. Meanwhile, this populous semi-arid, but irrigated region remains something of a Forbidden Land.

It remains to inquire how the presence of the French in Morocco is regarded by the natives themselves. It is difficult for a traveler to pronounce upon this important matter, but let us first consider the most obvious indications. To the town dwellers, the trading and manufacturing populations of Fez or of Rabat, French rule brought profound relief. It means security in the right to follow peaceful pursuits and enjoy the fruits of the vastly increased prosperity of the country. The capricious and tyrannical sultans who ruled in the past, and from whose exactions they suffered, never endeared themselves to their subjects of the towns.

There is another class in Morocco numbering at least 200,000 souls whose gladness at the change cannot be doubted. These are the Israelites. To them, the coming of the French is the first opportunity in hundreds of years to pursue their occupations free from injustice, cruelty, and indignity.

The tribes of the plains present another situation. They fought the French with determination from 1907 to 1912, as the area of conquest was steadily enlarged.

They have had their experience of warfare. The memory of defeat is vivid. They are probably well content for the present to take things as they are. The sedentary element plow their fields with a rude wooden implement frequently drawn by a camel and a little ass yoked together. They raise their wheat and other products as they have raised them in the past. They find a market for their surplus produce under a rule which, while foreign, is certainly stable. Two of these tribes around Taza, as has been noted, went over to Abd-el-Krim in the summer of 1925, but the method of coercion was extreme—the death of their hostages which Abd-el-Krim's harkas seized.

The Berber communities of the Atlas, now nearly all subdued, have made their submission reluctantly, and after long weighing of the issues. These communities are anarchistic in temper. They would prefer complete isolation. They have never welcomed any rule, least of any, perhaps, that of the sultanate of Morocco. They have yielded because they were persuaded that they must, or were forced to yield after the failure of their sharp conflicts with the French expeditionary columns.

The foreign population seems to mingle with the native on terms of amiability and confidence. There seems little question that the native trusts the French word whenever it is given. I had one evidence of this, of a minor sort, which surprised me. I was leaving Marrakech by auto-bus. It was an early hour of the morning; daylight had not fully broken. The bus left the station on the famous square called the "Assembly of Trespassers," and departed from the main route to

enter a native quarter. It was met by a half dozen
Moors who, even in the darkness, showed evidence by
their bearing and attire of belonging to a wealthy and
influential class. They had with them a woman whom
daylight disclosed to be young, and, so far as the face
of a Moorish woman is revealed, a woman who was fair
and of some social position. This woman, with many
protestations of friendship and of solicitude, the Moors
entrusted to the care of the chauffeur. She occupied her
seat throughout the hours of the long ride, undisturbed
by any attention from the European passengers of the
vehicle, and was delivered carefully into the hands of
her friends upon her arrival. This was doubtless a little
incident, but in a country where the person of a woman
is surrounded by such jealous guardianship, as among
the Moors, it had its significance in interpreting the
attitude of the natives toward the French.

No one can travel around Morocco and bear in mind
the repute of the country a few years ago; view the
surprising growth of such foreign communities as have
sprung up at Casablanca or at Rabat; observe the
roads, the magnificent bridges across rivers and barran-
cas, the solidity and beauty of French buildings everywhere, and not exclaim that the French have done
well. The only criticism which could possibly be passed
is that the French have expended money on Morocco
faster than the investment warranted; that foreign
traders and settlers have been encouraged to come in,
in numbers disproportionate to existing opportunities;
and that in their solicitude to make government impressive, to preserve the beauties of Moorish archi-

tecture, to protect antiquities, and to make solid and substantial their improvements of ports and their development of communications, they have outstripped the commerical development of the land.

There is something to be said for this critical point of view. A considerable debt has been laid upon Morocco, most of which is held in France and guaranteed by the French government.* The French believe that this debt is not disproportionate to the resources of the country, and, among other things, they point to the great phosphate deposits which are a government possession at Khouribega east of Casablanca. These deposits have not yet been worked at a profit, but they constitute an undoubted source of public wealth of vast proportions. The Protectorate would perhaps be glad to realize a great loan on this property and refund the public debt. American financiers, Mr. Paul Cravath and Mr. Wickersham, have visited these fields, and were perhaps invited to make a proposition, but no American financial aid to Morocco has been announced. The French are cautious about such matters, and they obviously like to keep the control of resources in their own hands.

* The debt of the Empire is as follows: Antedating the protectorate, a loan in 1904, of 62,500,000 francs, secured by the Customs Service; a loan in 1910, of 101,124,000 francs secured by the excess of the customs, the tobacco monopoly, and other items of revenue; under the protectorate, a loan in 1914-16 of 242,000,000 francs guaranteed by the French government; a loan in 1920 of 744,140,000 francs guaranteed by the French government, which in 1923 had been issued only in part. The first two loans are held in various foreign countries and constituted a foreign obligation which, under international administration, rested upon the country before the French assumed control.

In Morocco as elsewhere a certain priority of effort seems to be typical of the policies of French Empire. Commerce follows military and civil power. If colonial enterprises are not at once remunerative, they are at least never under the dictation of commercial interests, as they too frequently are in British colonies. The French put money into public establishments; they build expensively and solidly. Behind all this there can be seen an intention to give an unmistakable impression of the permanence of the empire which they are creating.

CHAPTER IV

MARRAKECH

THE important part played in the history of Morocco by the tribes living south of the Great Atlas,—the dwellers of the Sous and of the oases of the Oued Draa,—has been previously emphasized. Moroccan history, in fact, is largely the account of successive invasions from the south led by fanatical reformers, and followed by wild predatory bands from the deserts and mountains, who fell upon the rich cities of the northern plains, overthrew their rulers, and founded new dynasties of emperors. The strangest city of Morocco, and the largest, is the imperial capital which lies, in a sense, between the north and the south, —the mingling point of all the varied types of Moroccan population,—the city of Marrakech. It lies one, hundred and thirty-five miles due south from the Atlantic Coast at Casablanca. The ancient caravan route, if pursued further south, enters the Great Atlas by the valley of the Oued Nfis. In the center of this pass, at an elevation of several thousand feet, is situated the ruined city of Tinmal near the present mountain citadel of Kasba Goundafa. Here the celebrated Mahdi, Ibn Toumert formed the center of that religious movement which gave rise to the dynasty of the Almohades.

These wild mountain passes are the gates that pro-

72

tect Northern Morocco from the fanaticism of the south. Marrakech is the base from which these passes can be held. The city lies some fifteen or twenty miles from the foot of the Atlas mountains, which here rise to their grandest proportions. The spectacle of these mountains is superb. Through the clear desert air the eye can follow the rugged contours of the range for great distances to the north and eastward. The winter snows mantle them with white, and the turquoise sky gives a setting for their gray rocks and gleaming caps that is of unrivaled beauty.

The French had been fighting around Casablanca and in the great plain of the Chaouia for five years before the occupation of Marrakech was made. Then a savage massacre in 1912 drew the swift action of the French, and the city was captured by a column under Colonel (now Marshal) Mangin. The city is easily reached by automobile from Casablanca. The ride is over a plain which extends for more than a hundred miles. It is broken only by the course of a river or two, by an occasional small town or "kasbah", or by the wretched camps of Berbers. The plain impresses one for its vacancy and barrenness. At the termination of the drive the road rises between low hills. The bed of a sand-burdened stream—the Oued Tensift—lies before one, and beyond that, palmeries extending for many miles, at the southern end of which are the white walls of a great and ill-arranged city, above which looms the most striking architectural monument of North Africa—the famous tower of the Koutoubia. Behind lie the gray slopes and

gleaming peaks of the Atlas, and beyond them the illim-
itable azure sky. To the right, as the road approaches
the oasis, are rocky hills—the Djebel Gueliz—on
which the French Army, that captured Morocco, built
the customary strong camp, which became the permanent site of this southern post.

The region of Marrakech is frequently described
as desert in character, but, to one familiar with the
southwestern parts of the United States, the locality
does not suggest the desert, but rather an area of
seasonal rainfall, where moisture moves underground
rather than by surface streams, and where low brush
takes the place of the forests of more heavily watered
regions. The location of Marrakech on the north side
of the Atlas, rather than on the south, forbids its
being described as a Saharan city, but it is the northern
focus of the Saharan lines of communication, and its
history, its types of dwellers, and its commerce and
arts, are all related to the great south Atlas spaces
which reach to Senegal and the Sudan.

The manner in which Marrakech is supplied with
water is very curious. The course of the Oued Tensift
lies only a few miles from the city, but probably is too
unreliable a source of 'supply. In place of a diversion
of the waters from this stream, tunnels have been
opened through the immense talus or debris that lies
between Marrakech and the slopes of the Atlas. These
water tunnels are called "foggara" and they are in
some cases eight or ten miles in length. A point is
selected in the vicinity of the 'city at which it is re-

quired that a rivulet of water shall emerge. The tunnel is then driven southward for a distance of twelve or fifteen kilometers until it pierces water-bearing strata of gravel, perennially replenished by the melting of the Atlas snow beds. At frequent distances along the line of this excavation there are shafts, marked by mounds of debris from the excavation. I was informed that there are seventeen of these foggara, in all, of which number, ten were "dead" when the French occupied the city. All have now been re-opened.

The flow from these tunnels is considerable—enough to fill great ponds or reservoirs in the sultan's gardens, to supply a population of one hundred thousand people, and to maintain a considerable amount of cultivation at the southern end of the great palm groves, against which the city of Marrakech lies. From the exit of the tunnels the water is carried by ditches or *acequias* both through and around the city. These are dug gradually deeper to overcome the flatness of the plain, until, on the east and north sides, they are deep ravines in which lie sluggish pools, the resort of negro washerwomen and of animals.

The "palmerie" has a roughly triangular shape, the northern apex where it reaches the Oued Tensift being about sixteen miles from the city walls. It is said to include 86,000 palm trees. A doubtful tradition has it that these trees sprang from the seeds of dates which formed the food of a great desert army that one time laid long siege to the walls of Marrakech, and was camped upon this site. The trees while forming an exceedingly graceful mass are not individually striking, and the fruit is poor, and is used primarily for the feeding of animals.

Marrakech, while surrounded by walls and entered through gates, like other Moorish cities, sprawls in an unorganized way over the plain and occupies, with its gardens, a large area. The center of the city is the famous square called "Djemaa el Fna." The word is variously translated, but seems to mean the "assembly of trespassers" or malefactors. The spot has undoubtedly served as a place of execution, and for the exposure of the heads of decapitated bodies of the victims of the brutal rulers who could only maintain themselves in power by the constant exhibition of the fate of those who opposed or annoyed them. This great shapeless plaza is, at all hours of the day and evening, a place of gathering for the population of Marrakech, and for streams of visitors that flow into the city from the mountains and from the deserts. It is lined on two sides by shops for the sale of foods, animal forage, and the immediate necessities of journeying caravans. But the space itself is crowded with groups seeking the strange diversions of an African city. In one spot will be the snake charmers—wild, dark, frenzied men with long disheveled hair falling over their naked shoulders. The snakes which they manipulate lie in ugly coils at their feet. Three or four musicians with pipes, tambourines, and the inevitable African drum, add their medley of sounds to the shrieks and cries of the performers. Berber women, veiled and in long robes, always form the inner circle of the crowd that surrounds these repulsive exhibitions. As the snake-man reduces the serpent to a state of fascinated immobility, and picks up in his hand the asp, twines about his neck the great adder, or thrusts his own glaring face up to the very lips of the black cobra, the crowd not merely applauds, but lavishes upon the man a kind of religious homage. Hands reach forward to touch him, to get a smear of the spittle that covers his lips and face like a foam. The edge of his tattered garment is raised and kissed, and a strange unspeakable rapture appears to communicate itself from the repulsive performer to the crowd of his admirers. Occasionally a hardy fellow will allow the snake charmer to coil a serpent around his neck, or to dangle a little asp upon his palm, and he then receives the plaudits of the crowd. I made the mistake once of dropping a five franc piece into the outstretched contribution box of the snake charmer. He was carried away by delight at this unexpected munificence. He displayed my offering on all sides, lauded me as one of God's noblest and most generous creatures, then, as a touching mark of his esteem, insisted in crowding upon me the writhing serpents which he protested had been rendered docile. I escaped with some embarrassment.

As previously stated, these snake charmers belong to one of the numerous orders which flourish within the Mohammedan religion—the Aïssawâ—and have their headquarters at Meknes. At a certain time of the year a great gathering of these members is held. They parade with their wild music and their extravagant performances. They tear live serpents to pieces with their teeth and eat the flesh. Living sheep are similarly rent and devoured. For hours the city has an exhibition of that wild explosive fanaticism which underlies the impassivity of Islam. During the period of this celebration of the Aïssawa, the Israelites, of whom there are 15,000 in Marrakech, remain within the seclusion of the mellah.

In another part of the square one can see the dancing boys of the Atlas tribe of the Chleuh. They are comely little fellows of twelve to fifteen with plump smiling faces and round effeminate limbs. They are dressed and ornamented as women, their feet dyed with henna. Their dance is slow, dignified, and graceful, but its attraction is incomprehensible to a visitor from the western world.

At another part of the square are the story-tellers or reciters—venerable men with splendid voices, dramatic manner, and flashing eyes, who unfold for hours the mysteries of some ancient tale. Elsewhere on the square, camels kneel and little asses, discharged from their heavy panniers, pick among the rubbish for a few scraps of food. It is a place interesting not so much for the diversions which attract the throngs, as for the throngs themselves. All the races of Africa are represented in the crowds. They spread themselves over this famous meeting place—the descendants of Phœnicians and ancient colonizers, Berbers from the valleys and plateaus of the mountains, wandering Arabs from the plains, little companies from the oases of the Sous and the Draa, bringing with them the quaintly fashioned objects that they have for sale.

These include arms, powder-horns, leather work, modeled and ornamented on designs hundreds and perhaps thousands of years old.

In these crowds, the negro element appears as nowhere else in the cities of Morocco. These are slaves or the descendants of slaves, some of them maimed by disease or severities, some of them going about the endless and prolonged errands which make up the life of such menials, and some of them snatching a few moments of enjoyment by watching the diversions of the plaza. Many of them are old, bowed with the misery and labors of their years. Some are little naked children with joyless faces and large, tender eyes, slipping unobtrusively through the throng.

The life of the well-to-do class of Morocco still rests upon the ancient institution of domestic slavery whose eradication will be a matter of time. The French have done more than any people, except the British, to suppress slave marts, slave caravans, and the ferocious raids which supplied the human merchandise. Yet there is every reason to believe that a contraband traffic in slaves continues, and that unhappy Blacks from the Sudan in considerable numbers still make the dolorous traverse of the Sahara.

From the Djemaa el Fna one enters immediately the famous *souks* or market places of Marrakech. These markets, tortuous streets and open shops, are like the markets of Fez, but less orderly, less rich, and the men that labor, and the crowds that frequent them are poorer and more varied. But, in a way, these little factories and the shops which vend the wares are even more interesting, because more on a plane with the life of the people. I suppose that here is perhaps the best place in the world to study the curious arts of Africa. In the smoky smithies naked men, in semi-darkness, work on agricultural tools and rude arms; leather is tanned, dyed, and formed into pouches, saddles and harness; wool is woven; and the long burnouses and djellabas which form the outer garments of men are dyed, fabricated and sold. The foods, including grains, "kouskous", vegetables, fruits, spices, cakes and breads are varied, and in some cases savory. Like markets everywhere these places are an exhibit of the life and activities of the race.

On one side of the Djemaa el Fna stands a modern Moorish house which has a rather interesting history. It was built by the Sultan, Abd-el-Aziz, for the British officer, Sir Harry MacLean, known as the "Kaid MacLean", who, for years, was a military adviser at the Moorish court, and who was expected, perhaps, by the British government to assure the predominance of British interests over Morocco. His task was impossible, considering the proximity of the long Algerian frontier, and the determination of the French to secure a paramountcy in Morocco. The Anglo-British Agreement of 1904 terminated the long rivalry of these two powers for the control of Northwestern Africa, and in the history of this competition the rather extraordinary career of MacLean is a major episode. This building is now used as the municipal bureau or headquarters of that local control which the French general, re-

A QUIET STREET IN FEZ

LOOKING ACROSS THE HOUSE-TOPS OVER THE LOWER PORTION OF FEZ

BOAT BUILDING ON THE BANKS OF THE NIGER

BUILDINGS OF THE COMPANIE CONTONNIÉRE AT DIRÉ ON THE NIGER

sponsible for the jurisdiction of Marrakech, exercises over the administration of the city.

This French commander had been advised by headquarters at Rabat of my intended visit, and I was promptly called upon by a charming young man, who for several days was my guide and companion about the city. He was one of those soldiers of the World War to whom a succession of wounds has partially disabled the body, without impairing the magnificent spirit within. He had sought employment at Marrakech by reason of the climate which proved beneficial to his weakened strength. And in this strange city, and in the interesting activities of his employment, he had found something more than a physical improvement. He had discovered powers of appreciation of the artistic beauties of Marrakech, the freshness of its great gardens, the repose of its secluded interiors, the grave splendour of its mosques and tombs. He had lost an eye in battle, and he made this happy and illuminating observation: "When I had two eyes I never looked attentively at anything. But now that I have only one, I observe closely and with appreciation. I see beauty in ornamentation, in the color of gate and wall. I find new delight in the sight of things. Formerly I had no interest in art. Now I am learning to sketch and to draw."

With this interesting interpreter of Marrakech, I visited the famous Palace of the Bahia. The last notable sultan of Morocco was Moulay-el-Hassan, who ruled from 1873 to 1894. He came to the throne while still a boy. His affairs of government were committed to an extraordinary grand vizier named Ba-Ahmed, a man who was the son of a Jewess and of a negro slave. Among the remarkable enterprises of this powerful, subtle, and tyrannical minister is a vast palace which he decreed and executed. It extends over many acres, and is inclosed in gardens. It is a new thing, but built on purely native lines. It is perhaps the last great structure of its kind which a Moor will ever build. Without the haunting atmosphere of the Alhambra, it rivals the Alhambra in proportions and in the refinement of its decorations. Its creator assembled here the most notable artificers of the land—the stone carvers, men of skilled hands who can still chisel intricate patterns, traceries of exquisite delicacy, on the hard alabaster surface of walls and cornices, the shapers and carvers of cedar wood, the layers of tile, patterned in a profusion of tints into mosaics for floors, fountains and baths.

One enters the palace by a great gate, and is conducted through court after court, apartment after apartment, built around beautiful patios in which water plays, amid gardens of oranges and citrons. A growing amazement fills one at the greatness of the plan and the beauty of its execution. It does not appear that, once built, this great and ruthless mulatto ever filled these apartments and courts with his followers, his slaves, or his harem. It was sufficient satisfaction to create this thing, and then leave it to be wondered at and utilized by a foreign race. The present sultan to whom this property came has bestowed it upon the saviour of his country, Marshal Lyautey. At the time of my visit it was arranged for the occupancy of the Résident Général and of his staff, during those occasional periods when the headquarters of Rabat move to this southern city. But the European furnishings were of the simplest, and pains were evident to place nothing here that would be incongruous in its Moorish setting.

We also visited together the Saadian tombs. The Saadian rulers, who controlled the destinies of Morocco from 1524 to 1668, sprang from an Arabian colony which entered Morocco on the south, and settled in the valley of the Draa. It was a Saadian army which crossed the Sahara and fell upon Timbuktu, disturbing the peace and overthrowing the civilization of the Sudan which had reached its highest point in the 16th century. From Timbuktu this Saadian conquerer brought back to Marrakech the famous black jurist and scholar, Ahmed Baba, whose notable writings on the history of the Sudan were first discovered by Barth, during the enforced prolonging of his residence at Timbuktu in 1853. The story is that this noble black scholar lamented not his captivity, but only the loss of his great library of sixteen hundred tomes, which his unfeeling and barbarous master destroyed.

The French occupied Marrakech for five years before the existence of these remarkable tombs was suspected. They lie close to the great palace of the Sultan and the mosque of the Kasbah, but are sealed by dilapidated and unpierced walls. As the story was told to me, a group of workmen, under French over-

sight, had occasion to break a window through one
of these walls, and to their astonishment there was
revealed, within, a court of extraordinary beauty and
delicacy, supported by slender pillars of Italian marble
showing influence of Renaissance design, unique in
plan and beauty among the buildings of North Africa.
The tombs, which are great sarcophagi of marble, are
covered with inscriptions in the Arabic characters re-
lating the names and histories of the rulers who lie
buried within.

At the request of the sultan these tombs have now
been taken under French care, and the neglect of
centuries somewhat repaired. The mausoleum is entered through ruinous approaches overgrown with
weeds. Within, is a sanctuary of singular stillness, isolation, and of almost depressing beauty. The troubled
roar of a great and noisy city is subdued. There fills
the place something of that somber repose which characterizes Islam. My companion, whose recent years
had been so crowded with the roar of battle and the
shock of explosives, murmured with a kind of ecstasy:
"It is so quiet here!"

We drove out of the city and viewed its amorphous
outlines from the plain. Mile after mile of crumbling
parapet, red, like the soil of which it had been erected,
marked the ancient walls. White roofs gleamed here
and there within the disordered plan of the city. The
stony plains rose in a great sweep to the foot of the
towering Atlas, and mounds marked the long lines of
the foggaras. The mass of green palms disappeared
miles to the northward. The rocky hills of Gueliz,

crowned by the fortified camps of the Foreign Legion
and Senegalese battalions, guarded the new peace of
the land. But towering above everything, a sentinel
worthy to be planted at the foot of the Atlas mountains,
was the square, high tower of the Koutoubia. Towers
seem to be the finest expression of the architectural
aspiration, and of all the famous towers of the world
none surpass those of the Moors in the perfection of
their proportions, in the massive way in which they
rise straight and uncontracted from the ground, and
in the beauty of window, portico and minaret in which
their triumphs end. Koutoubia is the most splendid of
them all, the most splendid in the whole world, unrivaled by any tower of Italy or by any storied pagoda
of the Far East. It is built of hard stone and was covered in its upper proportions with faience of brilliant
hues that contrast perfectly with the dull tones of the
city over which it rises. Time, which has marred the
stone and tile, seems only to have enhanced the interest
and beauty of the structure. The Koutoubia was built
about 1184 by the great Almohad conqueror Yakoub
el Mansour, whose domain extended from the Guadal-
quivir in Spain to the Niger and the Senegal. It was
the ambition of this ruler to mark his empire by three
great monuments. Two of them were completed by
the same designer—the Koutoubia at Marrakech and
La Giralda at Sevilla. The third is the uncompleted
tower of Hassan at Rabat. All exhibit the same magnificent solidity. A great ramp traverses the interior
of La Giralda, and I presume of the others as well.
Four horsemen riding abreast could enter this ascend-

ing platform, turning a right angle at each corner, and
without changing their formation reach the upper pavilion of the tower nearly two hundred feet above the
ground. Koutoubia dominates not only Marrakech, but
the whole plain. Miles away it still greets the eye while
the city and oasis around it have disappeared.

Outside the city but close to it lie imperial gardens,
and particularly one, known as the "Aguedal". It is a
great orchard of olive trees, oranges, citrons, figs,
pomegranates, apricots, pears, and vines, surrounded
by a wall with gates and fortified bastions. The water
is brought in from two great tunnels and fills reservoirs hundreds of yards square. Lovely, light pavilions
stand on the paved banks of these calm pools. Built
first by the Almohades, this orchard was the pleasure-
ground of successive dynasties of Morocco.

Enough has been said to indicate that Marrakech is
a vital point of French empire in this land. Nothing
but a strong military force could make it secure. It is
in the residence of the great Kaid Glaoui and his allies,
through whose influence the turbulent tribes of the
region are controlled and the mountain passes made
safe. It will be increasingly the center from which
French achievement will operate on the tribes of the
mountains and the south. Hospitals and dispensaries
and modern schools already form new influences here.
They are agencies both to benefit humanity, and
to diffuse the repute of French achievement. Marrakech is a place of approach and observation for all the
restive leaders, mahdists, religious fanatics, avaricious
raiders, and contraband slave traders, and is counted

on to effect in these half-mad temperaments a change of conduct and a possible enlightenment of understanding.

Let me mention one other object that the visitor to Marrakech may see and reflect upon. It is the remains of an old stone bridge which crosses a little gorge where the city meets the palm trees. This bridge was built by Portuguese slaves—the debris of a Portuguese army which the Moors overthrew and made captives of the survivors. It was a defeat that brought to an end the hopes of predominance of a nation.that was once so incredibly active on the sea, which planted its forts and factories in the New World, on the coasts of Africa and in the Far East as far as Malacca, Formosa, and Macao. Morocco is full of traces of this nation once so great, and now so small among the states of the world.

The best place to view the remains of the Portuguese and to reflect upon their role, is Mazagan. Here the Portuguese fortified themselves in 1502. It was the last point to be occupied by the Portuguese in Morocco, and was their hold upon this land. The fortifications of the town are said to have occupied them for a third of a century. They stand unchanged by time. A complete wall surrounds the town which is perched on the cliff against the sea. The coast is open here, and the Atlantic beats against the walls of the fortress which overhangs the tiny harbor. The Moors have never occupied the old ville, but have built up a new town of their own outside the walls. The interior is the mellah or quarter of the Israelites, but it also shelters a small, European population, largely Spanish, and there is an old church, undemolished, dating from Portuguese rule, in which I found a little Franciscan friar lighting the tapers for service.

Perhaps the most remarkable thing in this town is the great cistern which underlies its streets and buildings. The roof of this reservoir is upheld by columns which in the subdued light serve to recall the mighty pillars of Mont Saint Michel. Into this enormous deposit of waters the rains were led, and a reserve formed against the sieges of the hostile tribes.

A considerable native trade centers at Mazagan. Coast steamers anchor off the shores. Lighters bring the cargoes to the beach. Skins and grains are exported, and I found a Spaniard who said he was engaged in the "good business" of exporting bones. These remains of cattle, camel, and sheep are strewn over the great plains frequented by the nomads, and they are collected for the sugar refineries at Marseilles.

Wandering along the sandy bit of shore, I came upon a company of natives who had passed a night there among their beasts of burden. The men were still lying on the sand closely wrapped in their burnouses against the chill morning air. Tumbled panniers and bales, and the debris of frequent encampments covered the ground, and a multitude of sorry camels and little asses knelt or stood patiently awaiting the resumption of their labors. Nothing more unpleasantly indicates the harsh nature of these natives than their indifference to their animals. Their camels are always emaciated and covered with bloody galls. Their little asses are invariably covered along the back and sides with bleeding wounds or vast scabs. No one who has loved the companionship and employment of animals can view these frightful little creatures without angry emotion. There can scarcely be greater contrast than there is in the treatment of animals by the Moors and by the more humble negroes of the Sudan. The colored race understands animals, and uses them well and tenderly. The gentler, more humane nature of the black, in this, as in other matters, stands out in favorable contrast to the morose, brutal and obstinate character of the Berber.

CHAPTER V

SOUTH OF THE SAHARA

IN the latter part of December, through the courtesy of the ship's commandant, I was able to embark with my camp equipment and guns on a vessel sailing from Casablanca for Dakar and the West Coast of Africa. The vessel was the "Kouroussa"—a little, old steamer of the Fabre Line which had been chartered by the French Government to "repatriate" a battalion of Senegalese tirailleurs. The accommodations were more than overburdened by this detachment of black soldiers, with their officers and other European passengers, but everybody was obliging. The cuisine was excellent. I spread my sleeping bag each night on the dining table of the little saloon, where, through the open port-holes, the fresh air of the Atlantic cleared out the stuffiness of cabin and hold. The obliging major-domo promptly found a bathroom on the main deck that was not working, in which he installed me and my effects. It was an excellent accommodation. I had space to overhaul my rifles and my impedimenta, which, in the difficult process of shipment from New York to Europe, and thence to Africa, had been following me for months. Thus I was the only passenger on board who had a whole room to himself!

It was really a beautiful voyage. The sea was undisturbed by boisterous wind. Our course lay only a few miles off the coast of Morocco, the Spanish Rio de Oro, and the great French Saharan territory of Mauritania, whose sandy shores broke the eastern horizon in a long level line. This sterile, and well-nigh abandoned coast is almost unvisited except by little fishing fleets, manned by Spaniards from the Canary Islands, or by Bretons.

The big black soldiers on the lower deck were always picturesque and amusing. Some bore on their breasts decorations and campaign medals. Their general behavior was excellent. With some of them traveled wives and little children, surrounded by the curious collections of small properties, which such families in the field or on the move seem to have the fixed habit of acquiring. There was just a suggestion of a Mexican army in this mingling of domesticity and martial order.

Each morning, just before daybreak, I arose and rolled my sleeping bag, hunted up a bath somewhere, had my cup of coffee and bit of bread, and then tramped the upper deck in a veritable ecstasy of pleasure. Dawn would come over the low shore of Africa, flooding the light clouds with beautiful colors. The sturdy little ship swung easily to the long roll of the sea. The air was cool and stimulating. My companions, black and white, were courteous and amusing. And I was at sea, bound for the Sudan and Timbuktu!

On the eighth day, soon after sunrise, we sighted the extreme western point of Africa, a low promontory, thrust into the ocean, which the Portuguese, in their persistent navigation of these waters, discovered fifty years before Columbus returned from his first American voyage, and named the "Green Cape", Cabo Verde.

Off this cape lies the tiny island of Goree, first occupied by the Dutch, and for centuries the entrêpot of the French for commerce and the slave trade. Under the shelter of the promontory is a harbor, which is already a highly frequented port for the shipping of the world. This is Dakar. It is the capital of French West Africa and the seat of the Governor-Generalcy. Dakar is a meeting point for ocean trade. It is about equi-distant from the North Sea, the Cape of Good Hope, the Rio La Plata and Hampton Roads. It may be visited, with little loss of distance, by shipping from North Europe or the Mediterranean, bound for South America or around South Africa. The continents of South America and of Africa draw near to one another in these latitudes and Dakar is the closest point of approach of the Eastern hemisphere to the Western.

From Dakar I journeyed by rail to Bamako, the capital of the French Sudan. Railroad building in Africa is in its infancy. Great projects, like the Cape-to-Cairo railway, which haunted the mind of Cecil Rhodes, are realizable and will transform this continent. Perhaps there is no more extraordinary conception than that which the French have under development, and which will be later outlined. For the present, all railroad lines merely start from the coast and carry one a brief distance into the interior. The railway communication from Dakar to the headwaters of the Niger has been long under construction. The last gap in this line has now been closed.

From Bamako I went down the Niger to Timbuktu. Then, setting out from Mopti, a place some days of boating up the Niger, I crossed the Sudan by way of Bandiagara and Ouahigouya, to Ouagadougou, an important post in the center of the well populated country of the Mossi people, and now the capital of the new French colony of Haute Volta, which was made a separate administration in 1919. Well established routes go southward from Ouagadougou through the Gold Coast, Togoland, and Dahomy. Through the courtesy of the Lieutenant-Governor of the Haute Volta, I was afforded motor transportation, which can be used during the dry season, and in this way I came out to the head of the short railway at Bouaké, and thence reached the Gulf of Guinea at Grand Bassam. At Grand Bassam I caught an Elder Dempster boat to Lagos, the capital of British Nigeria, and by the railroad which the British have built from the coast nearly to the northern frontier of Nigeria, a distance of 800 miles, I traveled to the city of Kano. Thence I returned to Lagos and took an express steamer for Plymouth, England.

My travel in the valley of the Niger and across the Sudan fell entirely in the winter months. This is the dry season. Very little rain fell until I reached the coast. The air at night was pleasurable and cool. Blankets were comfortable. Through the day the sunshine was warm but never oppressive. One should not judge a climate by its best season, but at that time of the year the Sudan seemed salubrious and delightful. I followed, rather carefully, the two rules of health which are insistently pressed upon one, that is, except when hunting in the late afternoon, I invariably wore a white helmet or "casque" when exposed to the sun, and I took five grains of quinine every day. I had no sickness or ill-feeling while on the continent of Africa.

Contrary to the livable conditions of the Sudan, the air became exceedingly oppressive after entering the tropical forest, and was particularly so along the coast of Guinea. Heavy rains set in. The air was excessively muggy and enervating. There was no relief night or day. I have spent more than ten years in the tropics, and have crossed the Equator in both hemispheres, and my feeling about the climate of the Guinea Coast in the month of March (when the season is supposed to be the worst), is, that it is more depressing and unhealthful than anything to be encountered in the Philippines, Malaysia, or equatorial America.

I was somewhat surprised, also, to discover that the advance of our knowledge of tropical hygiene seems unable to protect the lives of Europeans on the African coast. Death constantly hovers over the heads of the reckless livers in the little European settlements that dot the shore. Leaves of absence for recuperation in Europe are arranged with great frequency, and hardly a returning ship arrives with its full passenger list at Plymouth or Liverpool. The change of climate experienced between Sierra Leone and the Canary Islands, where cold winds from the north may be met, seems to be particularly deadly to the sufferer debilitated by the coast fever, and the sea here receives the bodies of countless broken men, whose African adventure is at an end.

It was an indescribable relief to escape from the coast of Southern Nigeria, cross the Niger again at Jebba, get into the broken hills and loose, thorny bush of the northern country, and, after the temperature and dampness of the Bight of Benin, meet again the brilliant but endurable sunshine of the dry, open savannahs of the Sudan.

The impression that I brought away, after my brief experience, is that the west coast of Africa is still, perhaps, the deadliest region of the globe to the white man; but that behind the narrow fringe of tropical forest there lies a vast region of quite a different character, where the white man may live in health and vigor, and where he might even successfully colonize, and that it is obvious that the closer one approaches to the Sahara the more healthful life becomes. I have never seen hardier or more robust white men anywhere than those French officers who have spent years in the arid spaces of the desert.

It is customary for travelers to describe in some detail the equipment they take with them, and frequently books of travel are loaded with pages and columns of articles cited as necessary. One can have a lot of fun in selecting and using camp equipment, and perhaps this is why one is tempted to set down his own. My experience is that one invariably takes too much; that baggage is a nuisance, a serious impairment of freedom of travel. And I am convinced that

the way to live in an inhabited country is to adopt, as
far as is practicable for a man of another race, the
manner of life of the natives. I carried most of my
"outfit" from California, and I believe there is no
place in which as serviceable and practicable camp
articles can be purchased as in the City of San Francisco, and no other equipment that represents as much
experience in judicious elimination as that which men
carry in hunting or automobile travel in the western
United States. But to the articles brought from home,
I added a curious little canvas folding cot of French
device which I picked up in Casablanca and which,
while good, was by no means the equal of our army
cot. An excellent iron table with three folding steel
legs, and a little iron chair, purchased at Bamako on
the Upper Niger, were better than anything of the
kind that I had ever seen before. Of food, I carried
to Africa none. At Bamako I obtained tea, coffee, cube
sugar, a few jars of *confiture* and about a kilo of
Roquefort cheese. This cheese got pretty black before
it was consumed, but a little bit of it was a welcome
addition to a meal at the end of a day.

Except for these things, I lived on the country. I
killed most of my meat—venison and magnificent fowl
which everywhere were abundant. The native villages
supplied rice, millet, potatoes, yams, onions, and even
tomatoes. Twice at French posts the friendly courtesy
of French officers supplied me with fresh vegetables
raised in the little gardens, which these French fron-
tiersmen invariably create wherever a new dwelling
place is established. And at Ouahigouya an official

gave me a beautiful basket of lemons, raised from trees which he himself had introduced into this part of Africa. From these ingredients, which were always abundant, my cook supplied me with satisfactory meals, and I felt the lack of only one thing—bread. I should add that my list of European-produced foods contained one thing more—a liberal can of fine olive oil. There is no better cuisine than that of the Mediterranean, which is based upon the olive tree, and a French-trained cook can be depended upon to employ it, but if he is unsupplied with olive oil, he turns to the African substitute, which is derived from the kernel of a sort of cherry tree. This substance the English call "Shea Butter" and the French "Beurre de Carité". The Negroes who produce this compound greatly esteem it, but its odor will drive an unwonted white man out of camp.

I had about 400 pounds of baggage. If I were going again I would carry only half as much. One must take several kinds of clothing, for on the coast the only rational or respectable dress is the suit of white drill, changed daily or oftener; and heavy clothing must be carried for the sea voyage on return. In the interior one needs only light underwear, riding breeches, flannel shirts, a sweater or good hunting coat, and a couple of pairs of good boots. The bedding roll should have sheets, a light pillow, and at least two blankets.

I had too many arms and too much ammunition. These included a Winchester—an old friend which I never used at all—and a light Browning rifle of small calibre which I bought at Marseilles for small game;

also another companion of more than twenty-five years, a Colt .41 calibre, single-action revolver which it is well enough to carry for personal security, and which is preferable to an automatic pistol because it will stand any degree of neglect and never fail its user. But I finally came to depend altogether upon a U. S. Army Springfield rifle, .30 calibre, beautifully made-over with a hand-made stock, pistol grip, and hunting sights, which was presented to me by friends on the eve of my departure. This rifle is adequate for every purpose, and I believe, as a sporting weapon, has no superior among firearms. The army ammunition, with steel-jacketed bullet, penetrates but does not rend, and is just the ammunition to use for guinea-fowl, ducks, or the magnificent game bird of the Sudan, the great bustard, or *outarde*. A special hunting ammunition for the Springfield, like the Lubeloy soft-nosed, "boat-tailed" bullet, has terrific shock power and, if well aimed, will knock down any animal in the world. I had, however, too much ammunition. A few hundred rounds of army ammunition and 80 rounds of soft-nosed bullets will give one daily hunting for many weeks, if judiciously used. I ruled out a shotgun, because of the bulky character of the ammunition, and after all, one does not travel in Africa to shoot small birds. For food supply the rifle is better. Fowl are very abundant, but they are also wary and one has usually to be content with shots at guinea-fowl or ducks at a distance of 70 or 80 yards. This is too far for a shotgun, but just right to make good sport with a rifle.

I had other equipment which I never used. A little

tent with canvas floor and fly was never pitched. If the weather proved stormy, native-built structures were available, and, in the Sudan, the huts are almost invariably clean and habitable, but, as I have already stated, my travel was in the dry season and permitted me, night after night, to sleep without shelter under the brilliant African sky. In addition to other things mentioned, I carried a light flat saddle, riding bridle, crop, spurs, and saddle pouches.

In this enumeration I am quite sure that I have given the maximum that a traveler in this part of the world ought to encumber himself with, and the list could be appreciably reduced without discomfort or hardship. With the sleeping equipment, however, should be mentioned, as indispensable, a closely woven net or *mosquitero,* made large enough to enfold the entire cot and with long strings at each upper corner, wherewith it may be hung.

I was alone, that is, without any European companion. This has both disadvantages and advantages. In setting out to cross the great continental interior, where conditions of land and people are unknown, it is true one becomes acutely conscious of his loneliness. He appreciates that there is only his single intelligence to direct things, and his sole will to carry the venture through, and that, under such circumstances, if one is disabled or falls ill, he is out of luck. Such thoughts obtrude particularly before the coast is left behind, and one is waiting for his transportation in the nostalgic settlements where men of his own race are gathered. At several such places, I admit, I desired the presence of a friend or a kinsman as a companion. But, very interestingly, once started into the interior all disquiet of mind disappeared, and left no shadow either of loneliness or apprehension. The journey at once appeared practicable, safe and enjoyable, and so continued until, after 2500 miles of travel, the coast settlements of white men were approached again, when, curiously, anxieties and homesickness returned. I think this experience is typical. Other solitary travellers in Africa, whose journeys were really prolonged, arduous and full of danger, as my journey was not, have testified to the same experience.—confidence, tranquillity, assurance, in the far interior; trouble of mind and hesitation to return, as the route neared the outposts of western civilization.

I tried to think out clearly a proper attitude of mind and came to this conclusion. There is something in the sunlight, the atmosphere, the wind of Africa that puts a great strain on the temper of a white man. Bad spirits seem to rise like the djinns from the opened jar and blacken the sky. Travel difficulties are magnified. Small obstacles and delays harass one until there may result a real feeling of malaise, an actual trembling of the limbs and explosions of temper. The pardonable stupidities of the native people, perplexed by peremptory and ill understood commands, may break down a white man's self-control and incite him to deplorable harshness.

There are two correctives to this white man's frailty; first, extreme care in making preparations, taking decisions, and issuing commands; second, the compulsion of the mind to be calm. The greatest virtue of a white man in Africa, and the most serviceable, is patience, and the power to be still when others are excited, startled, or enraged. Such discipline is especially needful if one has long tolerated habits of carelessness, impulsiveness, and procrastination. So I set a certain standard for my journey—that I would lose nothing, destroy nothing, and have no "incidents" or adventures, and, my travel affording no severe tests of my system, it worked perfectly. In fact, the patience, docility and devotion of these black people make for good results. Only a little dignity of deportment and considerateness of address are essential.

To this discussion I should perhaps add a word as to expense. Owing to the rate of exchange of French currency, travel in the French dominions was ridiculously inexpensive. The fare by steamer from Casablanca to Dakar was a thousand francs and, within the whole of French West Africa, both railroad and porter charges are fixed by government, and are exceptionally reasonable. So are all other costs and charges, and I wish to state that I was never once overcharged, disappointed in an account, or ever failed to secure exactly what I paid for, or contracted to receive. In these respects it was a most gratifying record of travel. In the British colonies the rates of expenditure are fixed upon a different basis, and, while fair enough, make costs high, and the same is true of steamship travel on express boats from the coast of England to British ports. There is a tendency in the British colonies to organize life so that there is a good deal of expenditure

that is unnecessary—something which the economical
instinct of the French avoids to the traveler's great
advantage. I can sum the matter up, by saying that
under present conditions, no American need hesitate
to travel in French West Africa because he expects his
total expenses of transportation and livelihood to exceed those to which he is accustomed at home.

The total length of my journey from Dakar to Timbuktu, and from the valley of the Niger, across the
Sudan to the Gulf of Guinea amounted to over 2,600
miles. In point of travel distances and the conditions
encountered, this trip might be compared with one
made by an American about eighty years ago (say,
about the year 1845) who, leaving Boston or New
York, could have gone by rail to a point on the Ohio
River 800 miles from the Atlantic Coast, and then
have gone down the Ohio and the Mississippi in a
barge or flatboat 500 or 600 miles to a point in Ar-
kansas territory; thence returned by river to St. Louis,
and from there traveled 700 or 800 miles across the
plains to Santa Fe, New Mexico. The military posts
and settlements that this American traveler of eighty
years ago would have found west of the Missis̓ippi,
would correspond to the French posts of the Sudan
and the Haute Volta; the parties of hostile Indians,
Comanches and Apaches, to the Tuareg; and the
traders and trappers of that day, to the French and
Syrian merchants who are penetrating the Sudan.

There are, however, important differences between
such a trip across the United States eighty years ago
and across West Africa today. The absence of govern-

mental organization on the American frontier contrasts with the strong French civil and military régime in Africa. On the great plains of the United States, the population was sparse and nomadic; in West Africa it is dense and largely sedentary. Control by the French in Africa is aided today, as the penetration of our own frontier was not, by the use of the modern inventions of the telegraph, the radio, the automobile, and the airplane.

CHAPTER VI

SENEGAL

THE Senegal River is a rather exact boundary between the Berbers and the Blacks. The white
population from the north, which, doubtless, frequented the Western Sahara at a time when the desert
was less desolate and even supported cultivation,
dominates the north of Senegal region to which the
French have given the name of Mauritania—that is
the land of the Moors. North of the Senegal, the common speech is Arabic or Berber. South of the river, it
is Wolof or Mandingo, and the population is negroid.
The "Moors" apparently represent different periods of
migration. Among them are tribes and families who are
called "Andalous," and whose ancestors seem to
have found their way to these remote deserts after
their expulsion from Spain. Obviously they have
mingled with the negroids. Their hair grows in heavy
ringlets, and their skin, like most dwellers of the
Sahara, is very dark, even darker than that of the
negro. Such Berbers as these extend inland from the
sea through the semi-desert country north of the Senegal and the Niger as far as the region of Timbuktu.
They bear a harsh reputation. It was among a tribe
of these people that René Caillié spent the long period
of instruction that prepared him for his visit to Tim-

buktu. It was into the hands of these nomads that Mungo Park fell north of the Valley of the Niger. Park could not forget the brutality he suffered at the hands of this race, and again and again in his narrative he repeats his indictment of their treachery, cupidity, and inhumanity.

Situated upon the banks of the River Senegal, the Berbers long barred the progress of white exploration up the course of this river. The Portuguese discovered the mouth of the Senegal in 1455, and on an islet at the mouth of the river, at Arguin, they built the first of those innumerable fortresses which line the coast of West Africa. The coast between the mouth of the Senegal and the River Gambia has been the most important foothold of the European for gaining the heart of the continent. It was two hundred years after the Portuguese settlement that the French succeeded to the empire of the Senegal, and in 1659 established Fort St. Louis. This post has grown into the city of St. Louis, the capital of Senegal, and was the starting point for French empire in the interior. Progress up the river, however, was long delayed. The appointment as governor, in 1854, of a great colonial figure, General Faidherbe, initiated the French plan of conquest. Faidherbe sought to reach the Niger, to gain Timbuktu, to open up these interior lands and to bring them under French sway. He did much to make this dream a reality. His first task was to punish the Berber raiders and confine them to the north bank of the river. He then carried his posts up the stream and erected the fortress of Medine upon its upper waters. He was op-

posed by a great negro leader, Omar el Haj, whose
character is still vividly remembered in the Sudan, and
who was succeeded by another opponent of the French,
the Almany Ahmadu.

The gradual progress of French forces went on for
years. The Niger River was reached in 1881, and the
fort of Kati, still a military headquarters, was erected
to guard the mountainous region between the Senegal
and the upper Niger. The fortress of Bamako was
built in 1883; roads were constructed; telegraph lines
laid; and the building of a railroad begun that should
connect the navigable water of the Senegal with the
middle course of the Niger. French conquest was occupied long with this hilly and populous region, from
which both these great rivers take their rise. In these
operations the black soldiers in the service of the
French grew into the trained, disciplined corps, now
generally known as the Senegalese tirailleurs. About
1880 the final struggle for the conquest of the Niger
began. The French had against them another famous
black, a mahdist or religious reformer who had made
himself master of a large area of the Niger basin.
This was Samory. Not until 1898 was Samory taken
prisoner. He was deported to the colony of the Gabun
where he died in 1900. Shortly before this Timbuktu
had been occupied, French forces had pushed far
eastward to Lake Chad, frontier agreements had been
reached with Great Britain and Germany, and the
development of the Sudan was at hand.

Meanwhile, the region of Mauretania had been left
in the possession of the nomadic Berbers. Subsidies

were paid to their sheiks to secure respect for the presence of the French, and to protect the caravans crossing the desert. After 1905 the French attitude became firmer. Punitive expeditions countered the treachery or insolence of the nomads, and desert centers, located in rocky groups of hills, like Tidjikdja and Atar were captured and held. The occupation of this arid region must have been a difficult species of warfare, involving the pursuit of raiding bands across interminable sands, the surprise of enemy parties in isolated oases, and the frequent relief of beleaguered French posts. As in Morocco, some of the most effective work that concluded this conquest took place during the World War, and the close of this war showed the French triumphant.

These military accomplishments made possible the further exploration of the Sahara. In 1920 a reconnaissance party under Major Lauzanne left the Mauritanian side, and effected a junction in the mid-Sahara with a similar party of *meharistes* coming from Algeria, under a notable desert explorer, Captain Augiéras. In the same year, 1920, Mauritania was raised to the rank of a separate colony.

Thus from the vicinity of the mouth of the Senegal, French effort pushed forward until it reached Lake Chad on the east, and effected communications across the Sahara to the north. These objectives attained, the effort now will be to consolidate French East African colonies into a single great possession embracing important portions of the coast and nearly the whole of the vast interior.

Until a trans-Saharan railway is completed, Dakar
will be the most important commercial center of this
empire. Its location on the western tip of Africa has
also suggested projects of a railroad connection northward along the coast to Morocco and Oran whereby
travel from Europe to Montevideo, or Buenos Aires
could be cut down by several days. Anyone can see
that the location of Dakar is important, and the French
have taken great pains, since its site was opened, to
provide it with harbor facilities and to connect it by
rail with the interior. The approach to this famous promontory is, however, disappointing. The cape is simply
a bluff, at most a few hundred feet in elevation, surmounted by a lighthouse, the Palace of Government,
and a few of the finer buildings of the town. If, in the
fifteenth century, there were forests here which suggested to the Portuguese to call it the "Green Cape",
these have disappeared, or are represented by little
except clusters of thorny chaparral. The coast-line, like
the entire shore south of the Atlas, remains low and
uninviting. The famous mountains of Senegal are hundreds of miles in the interior.

But the port once entered is impressive. The government, beginning about 1904, has executed good harbor
works—a breakwater, numerous piers, electric cranes,
and warehouses. The city and port are furnished with
an excellent water supply under pressure, which is
supplied either at the docks or by water barges to
ships lying in the harbor. There is a dry-dock, constructed by the French Naval Department, primarily
for the service of the squadron based on this harbor.

Our little steamer, the "Kouroussa," swung promptly
into its dock, its decks crowded with the eager groups
of black soldiers returning after their years of service
in Morocco. Formalities of debarkation were brief,
and in a few moments, salutations and farewells having
been exchanged, I was following my baggage over the
ship's side and into the custom-house. Here everything
was speedily cleared without charge or annoyance, my
guns and ammunition being held, until I could obtain
the necessary permission. This permission, I may say,
was most readily granted. It was sufficient on the following day to call on the Secretary-General and exhibit my letter from the French Minister of Colonies.
The secretary made a few inquiries as to the course
and length of my proposed travel, assured me, en-
couragingly, of its entire practicability, drew to the
front of his desk a narrow strip of paper, and on it
penned a few words descriptive of my several weapons
with the amounts and calibers of ammunition, added
a line giving me permission to hunt freely anywhere
in West French Africa for a term of months, and
handed to me this priceless memorandum without
charge. It was sufficient at once to clear my arms from
the custom-house, and while I was never called upon
to produce it, it was obviously considered all that was
necessary to assure my travel and hunting in the
interior.

Dakar is a new town, and like all the settlements of
western Africa, has lowly and dingy buildings, the
dwelling places of the commingled native and European
population. Of this population, according to a census

of July 1, 1921, 30,037 were natives, and of this number, again, 10,479 were black French citizens. The
European population was 2,403, all but 72 being of
French nationality. The streets are clean and well laid
out, in places shaded by trees, in others faced by
gardens full of tropical flowers. The offices and warehouses of the numerous mercantile establishments are
unsightly buildings with corrugated iron roofs, but
are full of traffic and activity. The only impressive
buildings are those constructed or used by the government, and as is the French practice everywhere, these
are spacious, imposing, and well made. There are two
or three hotels, not one of which can be recommended.
In one of them I was able to obtain a spacious, bare
room, where I made my headquarters for a week,
awaiting the departure of the "express train" for the
Sudan. The room opened by swinging glass doors onto
a concrete paved veranda facing the bay. It was agreeable enough to sit here and look out over the port, at
the docks crowded with ships and piled with mountains
of peanuts; at the bay cut with choppy white waves,
spreading out to meet the swell of the Atlantic; at
troops of white-clad negro laborers passing endlessly
along the water front. During this season of the year,
the coast of Africa is swept by a dry Saharan breeze
called the "Harmattan," which stirs up the dust in
little whirls, bangs doors and windows, disorders one's
papers, and has a harsh tonic effect upon the skin and
disposition. The air is filled with a species of African
kite—a brown hawk who carries on an unending pursuit of the lizards which expose themselves to the

warm sunlight upon roofs and walls. I cannot say that
the general life and atmosphere of the town were
engaging or pleasurable, but Dakar was endurable for
at least a time. The food in the hotel was abundant
but execrable. The lower floor was a bare ugly dining
room set with disordered tables, while under the shelter
of the veranda were the usual iron chairs and tabarets
for the service of the habitués of the café. The servants
were lean, dark Africans, barefooted and attired in
long smocks, who willingly but blunderingly discharged
the services of their profession. If there was *un petit
coin de Paris,* such as the French delight to create and
enjoy in their distant cities, I failed to discover one
that diffused any of the charm of the famous boulevards. There were, however, a few drinking gardens
which did not tempt a return call. In one of these,
while I loitered in Dakar, occurred a tragedy which
rather touched my heart. There was an American ship
lying in the harbor, one of the Shipping Board's constructions from the port of Long Beach of my own
state. Her crew were good-looking American lads of
the class recently recruited to supply the new American merchant marine. In a row which occurred in one
of these gardens of recreation, one of these boys was
severely injured. He was taken to the French Hospital
on the hill, where presently he died. The American
consul, the captain, crew, and myself attended his
funeral, which was a sad little affair, conducted by an
emaciated French priest, assisted by two colored aco-
lytes. We buried him in the cemetery down the beach,
under the swaying casuarina trees.

The American consul was the only citizen of the
United States whom I discovered among the residents
of Dakar, and he is the only representative of our
nation between Morocco and the Congo. Of the total
trade of French West Africa, France absorbs by far
the largest proportion, the greater part being in the
hands of French firms, managed by experienced men.
There is no such American agency at Dakar, although
American imports increased during the war, and in
1921 attained the unusual figure of fifty-four and
one-half million francs, the United States leading in
petroleum and tobacco, and taking a large part, during this and adjacent years, in the imports of coal.
It appears to be difficult, however, for American ships,
which discharge at Dakar to find return cargoes,
these having to be secured further eastward along
the African coast. Steamers of the United States
Shipping Board, operated by A. H. Bull and Company,
were making direct voyages from the United States
to Dakar and West Africa, but the competition
everywhere for trade is keen, and American participation on an important scale must await the time when
it is considered sufficiently important to American industry to develop it by the same expenditure of time
and means that have built up the commerce of European states in Africa.

I paid an interesting visit one day to the Island of
Goree, which lies only a couple of miles off Cape Verde
and Dakar harbor. Passage is made in a little harbor
steamer which operates regularly and conveniently
enough. I sat beside an old French colonist who expati-

ated at length on the variety and abundance of the fishing resources of the locality. I think he must have been a Breton.

The famous island of Goree is only a thousand meters long. It is quite solidly built over by substantial houses with long galleries and arcades, and by fortifications that date from the past centuries when Goree's importance was notable. Toward the sea the island rises in a bluff with steep descending cliffs upon which the surf breaks endlessly. At this high end of the island is the famous fortress of Saint Michel. It is a well equipped coast defense, and is garrisoned by a small detachment of French artillerists. At the foot of the bluff, mingled with the rocks and seaweed, I counted no less than fourteen ancient iron cannon, with their discarded gun carriages. They were really of great size and with calibers of perhaps eight inches. They had been tumbled over the precipice to make place for modern armament in this fortress which had guarded the settlement for centuries. At the opposite end of the island, facing the African coast, is a small circular fortification called "La Pouverelle." The old houses of the town are built of rough stone and roofed with tile. Many are now abandoned, and even falling into decay. Sandy streets, hardly twelve feet wide, connect the tiny squares of the town, and in the little *places* grow occasional fine trees, and in some of them is found a well. Cisterns, however, seem to be the main reliance of the town for water. These streets continue to bear names reminiscent of the past of Goree such as "rue des Dongeons," "rue des

Gourmets." The church has several statues of saints, two of them (a monk and a nun), representing blacks. The names on the pews appear to be those of Africans. There is, also, a small deserted mosque perched on the cliff beneath the fort, facing the sea amidst clusters of cactus and aloes. The "mejlis" of the mosque, or the alcove facing Mecca, is ornamented with bold designs in yellow and blue, and bears figures of the crescent and star. Old mats and goat skins lay on the floor, and a jar for ablutions stood in the portico. But no faithful came to kneel on the rugs, and the jar was empty.

The harbor, once so noted in West African trade, is a mere cove on the sheltered side of the island. It is a small sandy beach upon which stand old piers, a custom-house, and the office of the port. Above the sea walls rise terraces set with ancient dwellings, displaying graceful archways and deep balconies and porches. On the lower side the hook of the island surrounds the cove and ends with the graceful "Pouverelle" overhung with palms. The island was first occupied by the Dutch early in the seventeenth century who gave it its Dutch name, Gouree or Goedereede. The British captured the island in 1663, but it was retaken the next year by the redoubtable Admiral de Ruyter. The Dutch were expelled in 1677 by the French under the famous Admiral d'Estrees. Again the island fell into English hands, but was returned definitely to French possession in 1817. During all these centuries Goree was a great mart for the African slave trade. Here, in this little cove, once anchored the small cramped barks which carried the wretched negroes to the West Indies or to Charleston. Here, on this beach, this unfortunate merchandise was brought forth from the barracoons and marketed to the slavers eager to cram their holds with this pitiable cargo and take to the Middle Passage.

The suppression of the slave trade diminished the ugly importance of Goree, but long thereafter it remained an important depot of commerce on the west coast of Africa. This coast has few islands. During those long centuries, when all activities were predatory, an off-coast island represented security from native attack, comparative salubrity, measured against the fever-stricken line of the mainland, and a sort of "bridge-head" for European progress into the continent.

It would be a most interesting study to ascertain, if it can now be ascertained, what proportion of slaves reaching Haiti or the United States came from this port of Goree, for the slaves marketed here probably came, in large proportion, from the Sudan. The route for slave caravans lead up the Niger and down the Senegal or the Gambia to Goree. The type of slave recruited here, however, was not preferred in the New World. Compared with the pure negro of the Gold Coast, or of Calabar, the Goree slave was difficult to handle. He took his bondage hard; he resisted; he suicided; he died of melancholy. In other words, his white blood asserted itself against the docility of the negro strain. He was a negroid like our mulatto. Such types of slaves are easily recognizable in the history of

America. The physical type of the Sudan once seen on the old plantations has been described. They were perhaps the "brown niggers" of the South. Some characteristics of negro culture in America may have been derived from the Sudan. Names of slaves betray their origin. "Sambo" was a common American name. I had at least four "Sambas" among the men in my little caravans in the Sudan. "Cuffy" was another common name for American slaves. Is this possibly derived from the Senegalese name, *Kufu?* At any rate there is a possibility that that large proportion of white blood, which today characterizes the black race in the United States, was not wholly acquired in America, but was brought in part to this continent from Berber ancestry in West Africa.

Grim as is the past of Goree, its present character is wholly changed. It is one of the several towns of Senegal upon which the French government has conferred municipal status. Its black inhabitants are French citizens. Its mayor and municipal council are colored men. Its importance now is as an educational center, modest but important. Near the center of the town is the old *Place du Gouvernement.* Here the former palace of the authorities and other public buildings are used as public school buildings and to house the printing establishment of the government. There is a normal school and a technical or professional school and a school for the training of women nurses. The presence of young black students who form orderly groups about the squares within the shade of the old trees appears to be the only influence that now combats the general atmosphere of decline. Here, where for centuries our race inflicted such misery upon the black, the French government has determined that there shall be a center for his enlightenment and well-being.

CHAPTER VII

THE RAILROAD

RAILROAD development in French West Africa has proceeded slowly, according to American standards of enterprise, but methodically, and in accordance with a large plan of ultimate achievement. In one respect the French act in accord with American practice. They are ready to build railroads into undeveloped country because of the promise of developing settlement and transportation. Their present railroad building is confined to short lines, penetrating from several points on the coast, but all, seemingly, directed toward a common focus or junction in the interior. Their policy has also been to unite navigable rivers by connecting lines of railroad.

The oldest of their railroads is in Senegal, where a line 260 kilometers in length was completed in 1885, to unite the city of Saint Louis, at the mouth of the Senegal River, with the port and capital of Dakar. The Senegal River, during the months of high water, is navigable to European cargo boats for a distance of several hundred miles, or nearly to the cataracts of Felou, so that bulky, non-perishable commerce, at certain seasons of the year, can go by boat from the coast to the interior of this colony, there to be distributed. The most favorable point at the head of navigation of the Senegal is Kayes, where a considerable settlement has grown up and where, in 1881, the French commenced building a railroad line that now unites the upper waters of the Senegal with the Niger at Bamako. This railway through the hilly country of the Fouta Djallon is 494 kilometers in length. The desire to develop the interior of Senegal and obtain direct rail connections, independent of river traffic from Kayes to the coast, encouraged the French to build a trans-Senegal line from Thiès, 70 kilometers north of Dakar on the line to Saint Louis, to Ambidédi, a point on the Senegal, near Kayes. The realization of this project was long delayed, but was commenced in 1902. The last interval in the line was completed in 1923. Through traffic by rail from Dakar to Bamako commenced in December, and I believe that I was a passenger from Dakar on the first through train.

I left Dakar on Christmas morning, 1923, at about five o'clock. It was a cool dawn, lit by a late moon. The dry, winter *harmáttan,* was swaying the casuarina trees that surround the grounds of the *gare* and blew refreshingly in through the windows of the new and very comfortable cars. Beyond Rufisque, the track begins to cross a rather sandy and gravelly plain, covered with an interminable growth of brush, and with forests of baobab trees, which extend for hundreds of miles. These weird and grotesque trees, with branches that rapidly shrivel, like a palsied arm, are one of the characteristic features of West African scenery. Their appearance is grotesque and repulsive, rather than pleasing. They do not delight the soul and stimu-

late the sentiment, as do the nobler types of forest.
They seemed like things tortured and distorted by
some horrible experience. They are, nevertheless, ex-
tremly robust specimens of vegetation, and play a
considerable part in the economy of African life.

This broad interior of Senegal, while watered by
rains, is devoid of streams, and life can only be sustained here by the digging of deep wells. These conditions seem to have rendered it largely a desert previous
to French development. Only the nomadic tribes, accustomed to infrequent sources of water, appear to have
inhabited it. René Caillié records the sufferings of a
party in which he traversed this part of Senegal as a
boy. But the building of the railroad appears to be
stimulating settlement. Little towns and communities
are springing up. Progress in the extension of peanut
planting goes rapidly on. Game, accustomed in some
manner to exist far from water sources, abounds in
this bush, and with the digging of wells and with
security, larger herds of cattle are now brought in for
pasture.

All day long the train sped forward, through this
singular region, until, about dark in the evening, we
stopped for the night at the station of Tambacounda.
Here was a commodious station hotel, which the
French describe with the less pretentious title of
"buffet." Good meals were served and comfortable
repose was had in a clean, well aired, adobe room. The
place was surrounded by shrubs and trees and, an hour
or two before daylight when we were roused, was suf-

fused in beautiful moonlight. As on the previous day, the air was cool and agreeable.

The little station houses along the line are new, are built usually of brick or concrete, and seem to be in charge of native station agents. Shortly before reaching the Senegal River, the fine stream known as the Faléme is crossed. While the waters had fallen to the winter level, the Senegal River was nevertheless a beautiful sight, flowing between high banks, bordered by fine trees, and its current animated by low-draft, native sail boats, which continue the active navigation of the river when its waters become too low to admit steamships.

Further up the valley of the Senegal, the cultivation of the *sisal* flourishes, and I saw one large and thriving plantation. We made the crossing through this pictur- esque region between the Senegal and the Niger in the night, and I could gain only an imperfect impression of its interest. We arrived early in the morning at Kati. Here is the principal military post of the Sudan. It is a beautiful locality. Water is plentiful. Well tended gardens are everywhere. The place has an atmosphere of military order and native well being. From this point the descent is relatively rapid, through forested hills, until the landscape opens out into the magnificent river valley of the Niger at Bamako.

This railway line into the interior, which has just been traced, has a total length from Dakar of 1290 kilometers or over 800 miles, and is the most important railroad enterprise in West Africa. Its union of the coast with the services supplied by the two great African rivers affords certain, though somewhat long, combined water and rail transportation with the interior.

A second railroad line has been built from Konakry, the port of French Guinea, south of Dakar, to the navigable waters of the Niger at Kankan, thus affording another link in the network of communication which centers about the Niger. A third railroad penetrates the forest of the Ivory Coast from Abijan, on the lagoons back of Grand Bassam, and at present affords service for about 130 kilometers to Bouaké, where the country begins to open from the tropical forest into the freer spaces of the Sudan. Construction is being continued northward toward the Kong hills. Further east, French railways run north through Dahomey for about 80 kilometers, and these are paralleled by the German-built line in the French mandate of Togoland, from the coast at Lome to Atakpamé.

These several routes, starting from different points on the African coast, are capable of being brought together at some central point in the Sudan, and the most likely point to be fixed upon would seem to be the Mossi capital of Ouagadougou. This place could be connected by rail with either Mopti or Bamako. The latter route traverses the populous and important region which finds its center in the African city of Sikasso. From Ouagadougou, also, communication may be developed eastward to the Niger at Say or Niamey, affording approach to the British territory of Northern Nigeria, but I think the French project goes further than this and contemplates carrying such a route north of Nigeria through the *Territoire Militaire du Niger* to Lake Chad. The French mind, obviously, is occupied with the desirability of binding up the West African possessions through the interior, and by the creation of a future interior railroad junction, toward which French traffic from all directions will converge. Again, the considerations that support this project may be military and political. Beyond the union of French West Africa, through the interior, the mind moves on to a railway connection around Lake Chad, with the other African governor-generalcy, French Equatorial Africa.

But the French conception does not stop with these ends. It considers a railway connection from North Africa to the Sudan, across the Sahara, and this brings us to, perhaps, the most fascinating and unusual problem of communications in the whole world.

The Sahara desert surpasses all other waste and arid regions of the earth, both in its immensity and in the extreme degree of its sterility. From the Atlantic to the Nile, it has an eastern and western extension of perhaps 3200 miles, while the distance across it varies, according to the route taken, from 800 to 1400 miles. This represents a total area of 3,500,000 square miles—the size of Europe, including the Scandinavian peninsula.

Geological evidence indicates that, as late as Quaternary times, the Sahara was fairly well watered and supported life. It was traversed by rivers and streams, the fossil beds of which constitute the "wadis" or valleys which radiate from the mountainous regions of the

Sahara, and which are the eroded beds of rivers and streams long dead. In the geological period preceding the present, the Sahara appears to have formed a bridge between the plant and animal life of the tropics and of the Mediterranean. There are some extremely curious examples of the persistence of these types of life. Tropical fishes still exist in some of the subterranean streams and lake depressions of the north Sahara, and living specimens of the crocodile have actually been taken in shallow waters north of the Ahaggar mountains. The desiccation is probably more complete than it was in the times when the Romans penetrated the desert, and when the caravan routes across these areas of desolation were first discovered and marked down.

There are some persistent misapprehensions in regard to the Sahara. One of them is a current belief that it lies below the level of the sea and might even be flooded from the ocean. While there are limited regions of extreme depression, the Sahara, as a whole, appears to be an elevated arid steppe or plateau, which rises at certain points into mountainous regions. The most important of these is the Ahaggar, a mountain massif of about the area of the Alps, volcanic in nature, with peaks that rise to 8,000 feet, and occasion a limited amount of precipitation. At times, the Ahaggar peaks even have caps of snow. The Ahaggar lies in mid-Sahara about 900 miles south of Algeria and about 600 miles northeasterly from the great bend of the Niger.

Southwest of the Ahaggar is another mountainous region, called the Adrar of the Iforas, and to the southeast, another similar region, the Aïr. Like the Ahaggar, these elevations receive just enough intermittent rainfall to make them habitable to an exceedingly limited human population.

In the dry courses between these mountainous districts, there are, however, ancient wells and waterholes, days of travel apart, which mark the stages of the caravan routes across the desert. From the southern slopes of the Atlas mountains, the wadis carry subterranean waters for hundreds of miles and, at times, are even filled with freshets and running streams. These conditions give rise to the north Saharan oases, the most remarkable of which is that of the Wadi Saoura. Here, in ancient times, water was gained through tunnels and wells, which are today supplemented by artesian wells driven by the French. The population of the oases is mixed with negro stock, brought in from the south, but basicly it is of Berber blood. The total population is put by Professor Gautier at 60,000 souls, but besides the sedentary, village-dwelling inhabitants of the oases, the Sahara has another and still more amazing race of inhabitants, the famous "veiled men" of the desert, the Tuareg, who hold the mountainous areas of the mid- and south-Sahara, and who are the desert men par excellênce. Their possession of the camel enables them to know the desert, and to find their way across with a skill that is marvelous, while the extreme paucity of their resources of life has made of them raiders of caravans and pillagers of the oasis villages. Their long unapproachable home in the Ahaggar is the region celebrated in the romantic novel *L'Atlantide,* by Pierre Benoit.

The historic caravan routes across the Sahara are several. The best connects Tripoli through Murzuk with Lake Chad. It was the route followed by Dr. Barth in 1850, and by which he returned in 1855. Water and herbage exist along this passageway in sufficient amounts to permit its passage by horses. On all the other routes the camel is indispensable. The routes from the south Atlas oases pass by way of Ahaggar and, from this central point, either go south to the Niger or southeasterly to Aïr and thence to Zinder or to Lake Chad. The still more westerly route between Timbuktu and Morocco will be described in connection with an account of the salt mines at Taodeni. It was the route followed by René Caillié and by Lenz.

These routes, long frequented by the Berbers, have only recently become known to the French. In 1881 the exploration of the Sahara received a decided check, through the massacre of the Flatters' Mission, at Gharama in the Ahaggar. This tragedy produced an unduly powerful impression of the invincibility of the Tuareg, and of the difficulties incident to their subjugation. For twenty years French advance was stopped, and the mid-Sahara left a field for romantic fancy. The spell was broken in May, 1902, by the remarkable pursuit of a raiding party of Tuareg, by a Lieutenant Cotterest, with a small force of desert camel men. The chase led him to the very heart of the Ahaggar, where he fell upon the raiders at the wells of Tit and destroyed them. The mystery was dispelled, the reputation of the Tuareg vanished, and the French began a succession of reconnoissances which resulted in the opening of the entire mid-Saharan region to their information, the establishment of posts, and the development of a corps of French officers and meharistes adequate to assure protection against the desert tribes. Cotterest's adventure had been preceded, however, by the extraordinary Foureau-Lamy expedition, which left Ouargla October 23, 1898, and reached Zinder, November 2, 1899. In this case a company of Senegalese infantry of 250 men, with their officers, accomplished the crossing of the Sahara on foot. The further exploration and conquest of the desert required a great organizer and leader and he was found in the person of Laperrine.

In considering the French project of bridging the Sahara by railroad, there is another misapprehension which must be cleared from the mind, namely, that the desert is a continuous mass of drifting dunes of sand. The sand-dunes—the *erg* or *igidi* of the Berbers—are found over considerable portions of the desert, but their positions seem relatively stable and camel trails pass between the great windrows of sand, while most of the Sahara is a stony, bare, wind-swept plateau, which offers a solid basis for roadways or for rails. The actual area of pure sand is relatively small.

While it is unlikely that water can be extensively developed, except in the rare spots where wells now exist, it can be carried along a railway, and there would seem to be no physical obstacle to prevent the building of a trans-Saharan railroad line except the expense. The French have long studied this project from the standpoint of its political, military and economic advantages. There are opponents to its practicability and usefulness. Nevertheless, the project advances, and in 1923 it was approved by the Superior Council of National Defense. A private French railway company has undertaken to make the definitive survey. So there is little doubt that this long-considered plan of a trans-Saharan railroad is making advances towards its realization.

France already has two railroad lines entering the Sahara from the Mediterranean. One of these departs from Mascara a short distance from the Mediterranean port of Oran, goes south to Ain-Sefra, thence southwesterly as far as the post of Colomb-Bechar, on the southeastern frontier of Morocco. From here goes the important caravan route southerly and southeasterly through the oases of Touat and Gourara to the central Saharan regions of Taourirt and In Salah. It is approximately 600 kilometers by the existing railroad from Mascara to Colomb-Bechar, and 600 kilometers more by the caravan trail from there to Taourirt.

The other railroad from the Mediterranean goes south from Constantine, through Biskra, to Touggourt. From here the caravan route goes south-southwest through Ouargla and Hassi-Inifel, to In Salah. This route is somewhat longer than the one by Colomb-Bechar and Touat. South of In Salah, lies the very center of the Saharan desert, the Ahaggar. From here the route leads on through the Adrar des Iforas, where the

THIS IS THE LANDING PLACE AT WHICH THE SLAVING SHIPS ANCHORED

The "Pouverelle" is at the extreme rear of the picture

TRAVELLERS' BARGES (CHALANDS) ON THE NIGER RIVER
My boat christened the "Oualata", after an oasis town west of
Timbuktu, is the one farthest from shore

THE SENEGAL RIVER AT AMBIDEDI

boundary between the Algerian jurisdiction and that of the French Sudan is crossed, and reaches the Niger at Bourem, about 250 kilometers east of Timbuktu. It is probably the Oran, Colomb-Bechar, In Salah, Tamanrasset, Niger River route that will be preferred. It may be somewhat shortened by leaving Tamanrasset to the east and crossing a completely sterile area, which was navigated by automobiles of the Gradis expedition in 1923. The point at which the Niger will be reached will be Tossaye, where the course of the river is constricted between cliffs, and where the most practicable point for bridging is to be found. From here, as above stated, the railroad would connect with the junction of the West African coast railways at Ouagadougou. The total amount of additional railroad to be built will amount to at least 2,000 kilometers, and is calculated to require fifteen years to build. Its completion would shorten the distance from the Niger valley to Marseilles across the Mediterranean, to a total of about 3,300 kilometers. It would unite Europe and North Africa, by the shortest possible journey, to the Sudan, West and Central Africa. It would make possible the economic exchange of the manufactured articles of Europe and the raw products of the most highly developed region of Africa. It would enable France to bring to her succor in Europe, in at least considerable numbers, the fighting man-power of the Sudanese, and it would unquestionably consolidate the political position and authority of France over a vast region of the continent. Viewed in this light, the Sahara appears something like an inland sea, the shores of which are almost entirely in French hands. It is a difficult sea to traverse, perilous and expensive to navigate under present conditions, but of potential value, none the less, because it may be bridged.

The Saharan railroad project has been brought nearer by the traverse of the desert in automobiles. There have been three of these so-called "auto raids." The first was that accomplished by a party organized by the Citroën Automobile Company, in December, 1922-January, 1923. It was handled by a member of the Company, M. Harrdt, and led by a young officer, the son of a French general, and himself a Saharan explorer and commander of meharistes—Lieutenant Audouin-Dubreuil. With six cars fitted with tractors for overcoming difficult ground, this party left Touggourt and drove, by way of Tamanrasset, to the Niger, in eighteen days. The feat was then duplicated by the Gradis expedition, using Renault machines and special tires, and again by the second Citroën expedition, which made the run between Colomb-Bechar and Timbuktu in six days' time. So encouraged was M. Citroën by the success of these demonstrations that he announced the establishment of a tourist service across the Sahara to Timbuktu, a project which, it has now been announced, has been temporarily abandoned because of the hostilities of the desert tribesmen. Nevertheless, it is apparent that modern inventions are about to replace the laborious camel traverse of the Sahara, and another of the forbidden areas of the world has been opened to the knowledge, travel and occupation of the European.

CHAPTER VIII

TRAVELING today over the newly completed French railroad, one reaches the Niger Valley at Bamako. To the northward of this well-laid-out town, and several hundred feet above the level of the river, there rises a beautiful mesa on which have been constructed the fine residences and offices of the Lieutenant-Governor of the Sudan and his staff. Here I was most hospitably entertained. The view from this summit is interesting and inspiring. Below, and extending for many miles, is the shining stream of this wonderful river, coming toward one out of the southwest from the hilly country of Gambia and disappearing miles to the eastward on its mysterious course into the interior of the continent toward the Sahara.

The Niger must count among the great rivers of the world in length and in volume. It is just a little longer than the Mississippi. It rises close to the Atlantic Coast, penetrates the great desert and then, bending southward, is lost in the mangrove swamps and deltas of lower Nigeria. Its extraordinary course made its true character long a matter of surmise and erroneous conjecture. It was thought to end in the Sahara, as it probably once did. It was held by others to be one of the sources of the Nile. Later, it was believed to be the upper course of the Congo. As late at 1829, General Sir Rufane Donkin published "A Dissertation on the Course and Probable Termination of the Niger," in which, by a great deal of reference to writers as widely separated as Herodotus, Ptolemy, and such modern travelers as up to his time had penetrated the Sudan, he came to the conclusion that the Niger was the source of the great inland sea of Lake Chad.

The long course of the Niger is twice broken by rapids, impassable by boats of any description. The first of these begin at Bamako and extend some fourteen miles to Koulikoro, which thus becomes the head of navigation of the middle Niger. The French railroad has been extended from Bamako to Koulikoro, thus providing continuous rail and water transportation to Timbuktu and beyond. Four hundred and thirty miles below Timbuktu, at Ansongo, the navigation of the river is again interrupted by rocky barriers, and for 250 miles the current is dangerous, flowing through rocky passes with great velocity and frequently being lost in a labyrinth of reefs, rapids, and islands. Even below this point, the Niger only becomes navigable when it enters what is now British territory, from Jebba to the sea. In its lower portion the Niger receives the waters of the Sokoto and the Kaduna, and lower down, the great stream called the Benue. After it enters the tropical forest it breaks into innumerable mouths, occasioning the delta of the Niger which extends along the swampy coast for 120 miles.

It is apparent that the Niger, set in motion by the torrential rainfall of the mountains close to the Atlantic

Coast, and forming a great stream, flowing, not toward the sea, but toward the interior, has in some manner broken through the range of low barrier mountains that enclose Africa like the rim of an upturned saucer, and reached the sea at an unanticipated point. What apparently happened in the history of the river was this, the Niger was at first a stream without an ocean outlet. It emptied into a great depression in the vicinity of Timbuktu and formed a marshy lacustrine region, like that of Lake Chad. Then another stream, at first an entirely separate river but now the lower Niger, flowing from north to south into the Gulf of Guinea, eroded its way backward through the low barrier of hills until it tapped the lake region which the Upper Niger had formed, drained off this inland sea, captured the Niger proper, and there resulted from two river systems, one.

The watershed which at one time separated what were then two streams is today represented by the cataracts of Ansongo and Say. What was formerly an interior sea, lacking outlet, is represented today by extensive depressions and sloughs on the northward bend of the Niger before it reaches Timbuktu. The largest of these are Lakes Debo and Faguibine. But at time of high water, the force of the Niger breaks up into many channels, and the current is diverted backward as well as forward, until these ramifying and extensive depressions are filled, and a level of submergence attained. After the rainy season ends and the flood in the Upper Niger subsides, these lakes and marshes, *maragouts* the French call them, slowly empty, and the lower course of the Niger becomes swollen with the flood. The result of all this is that, while high water in the Upper Niger comes with the summer rain storms, high water at Timbuktu does not occur until December, and the flood does not reach the Lower Niger until the middle of spring.

The practical effect of this is likewise surprising. There is sufficient depth of water for light-draft river boats between Koulikoro and Mopti, where the stream bends sharply northward toward the Sahara, in the summer and fall, but such boats cannot reach Timbuktu until December, when the current is already rapidly falling below Koulikoro, and the return trips from Timbuktu to the head of navigation at Koulikoro cannot be deferred later than early January. As one Frenchman expressed it to me, the Niger has *"un régime tout à fait special."* It thus results that in spite of its impressive length, about 2600 miles, it is possible to use steam vessels even on the middle Niger only for short periods of the year.

The French have built a number of small, very light-draft river steam boats, the best of which, the *Mage,* contains staterooms and accommodations for a number of people, but the main reliance is upon barges, *chalands,* of differing sizes, now usually built of iron. Each of these is in charge of a black man with one or two associates, and they can be poled, sailed, or towed. On certain of these barges a rude but habitable little cabin is placed, in which a passenger can make himself most comfortable. It was such a little boat as this that was placed at my disposal by the Navigation Office at

Koulikoro. The *patron* was a Fula man, named Baba Djalu, an oldish fellow, spare of frame, with a thin amusing chin whisker hanging below a mouth from which most of the teeth had disappeared. He camped in the bow, and had a little fo'c'sle in which he kept his property, which consisted of a wooden box with a lock, a mat, a sheepskin, several gourds filled with prepared meal, called *kouskous,* and above all, a supply of kola nuts which, lacking teeth, he was forced to grind on a little grater made of a piece of tin. At the rear of the boat his companion, a *Kado* man named Alibani, perched on a sort of quarter deck, where he operated the iron rudder. On this little deck, too, were the mud stove and supply of fuel, which could be tended through a window in the rear of the cabin.

The cabin was eighteen feet long and six feet four inches wide. My tent floor partitioned off the rear end for my cook and his kitchen, leaving sufficient space in front for cot bed, table, chair, guns, and saddle. On the walls I hung clothing and clothing roll, toilet case, and other impedimenta. A box nailed to the wall held books, maps, papers, and tobacco. On the wall, too, I hung my American flag. It was a jolly little accommodation, and really one could ask no better way to traverse a great river of inexhaustible interest than in a house boat of this character.

It remains for me to speak of my cook. At Dakar the Governor-General advised me to engage no boys on the coast, but to get the far more reliable type of servant to be found in the interior. At Bamako through the request of the Governor, the administrateur

summoned for inspection a bright, cheerful young
Black who bore the name of Anadí Talori. He came
from a far-distant eastern region of the Haute Volta,
the district of Fad 'n'Gourma, but he had been in the
employ of French officers for four or five years, could
speak a little French, and was recommended to me
both for character and proficiency. I was so taken with
the chap that I engaged him on the spot, and told him
to equip himself and be ready to leave for Koulikoro
the following morning. Later in the day he came back
with an apology and an explanation. It seemed, he said,
that when he engaged himself in the morning to travel
with me down the course of the Niger and across the
Sudan to the coast of Guinea, he had momentarily for-
gotten that he was a family man. He had a wife and a
petite bébé whom absentmindedly he had overlooked.
He was puzzled as to what he should do with them,
and even suggested that perhaps he had better retire
from my service. Time was so lacking, and I was really
so anxious to take this boy along, that I decided to risk
everything and embark him with his entire family. The
wife proved to be a small, comely young woman, well
behaved enough and usually merry, with a four-year-
old baby girl, who likewise was well behaved. We
parked them with friends at Mopti before continuing the voyage to Timbuktu, and left them again
at Ouagadougou, to which point my cook, ultimately,
I hope, returned. They were rather amusing than
otherwise, and I never tired of observing the extreme
attachment existing between this colored mother and
child.

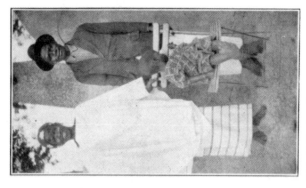

MY COOK, ANADÍ TALORI WITH HIS "FEMME," AND "LA PETITE BÉBÉ"

THE BAOBAB TREE

A VILLAGE ON THE BANK OF THE NIGER BETWEEN KOULIKORO AND SEGOU

We got away from Koulikoro on the afternoon of December 30, 1923. There were seven or eight barges lashed together, my own being the rearmost, and these were in the tow of a little flat-bottomed vessel, which bore the distinguished name of René Caillié. The captain, engineer, and crew were all blacks. The decks of the small steamer and the roof of the shelter were piled high with logs which constituted the fuel. Two of the barges were house-boats like my own, and these were occupied by a small party of officers and *sous-officiers* bound for Timbuktu, a couple of civil servants, and a trader or two for points down the. river. The other barges were loaded with freight, and their decks crowded with native passengers.

We were fourteen days making the voyage to Kabara, the port of the mysterious Saharan city. But the time was none too long. The winding shores of the river presented a succession of charming little pictures. The whole valley of the river teams with life. The waters abound in fine fish, to catch and market which is the province of one particular river tribe, the Bosos. Crocodiles sprawl on the long yellow strips of sand, and offer inviting targets to the rifle, though I saw none that approached in size the formidable, predatory "caiman" of the Philippines.

Water-fowl were innumerable, and included ducks and geese of remarkable size and beauty. A specimen of one of the larger species of ducks measured twenty-seven and three-quarter inches from tip of bill to end of tail, and fifty-three and one half inches between the tips of spread wings. This species is black and white, but carries a beautiful splash of scarlet over the back, with a red spot as big as the palm of a hand on the breast. Dressed, it was almost the size of a young turkey, and hardly less tender and edible. Pigeons, doves, partridges, and guinea-fowl abound in the trees and brush along the shore, and occasionally roe-bucks may be seen coming to or returning from water. Once or twice a day we tied up on the banks alongside of great woodpiles, where the fuel of the René Caillié was leisurely replenished. On these occasions I would go hunting through the sparse timber, or explore the streets of some little town or village.

These frequent settlements are interesting and really charming. The valley of the Niger has its own type of architecture,—mud walls, windows latticed by adobe bricks set in geometrical patterns, ornamental doorways, and particularly, low mud minarets thrust up like the blunt stub of a fat cigar above the roofline. These singular little minarets always carry the timbers used to support scaffolding built up in their construction and necessary for their repair, and these timbers stick out in all directions like pins from a perpendicular cushion. Above the roofs of the village rise great thorn trees, palms, and sometimes the grotesque baobab tree.

For a mile around such communities lie the millet fields, at that season of the year in stubble, but the main activities of the village were always on the shore. The waters of the Niger were falling, and in the damp, fluvial slopes patches of garden verdure were springing up, including little areas planted to tobacco. The shallow waters of the stream in front of every town were always crowded with innumerable bathers and women were ceaselessly washing, scrubbing their utensils, or filling the water gourds. The population of the Niger valley is a mixture of the many stocks and tribes of this part of the Sudan. Yet the system of assignment of trade or occupation to special tribal groups or classes still persists, and this is especially marked in the cattle industry, which, over many hundreds of miles, is practically confined to one singular, semi-nomadic people, the Fula or Peuhls. Some writers connect this people with the ancient Egyptians, but they are probably one of the mixtures of Berbers and blacks. They extend from Senegal to the Nile. Their hair is smooth or falls in ringlets and is never woolly. Their faces are oval and the features often are delicate. They are virile, warlike and in Northern Nigeria, where they conquered the Hausa kingdoms, they showed real talent for government. They were always to be seen along the shores of the Niger, bringing their herds of spotted, long-horn cattle down to the banks for water, or stabling their animals in rude camps, either by a picket line attached to a four-foot, or within little *zaribas,* or thorn bush-corrals.

At certain points on the river the settlements rise to the dignity of historic towns, such as Segou, Mopti, and especially Djenné, once the seat of a famous empire, which, being off the Niger and on its important affluent, the Bani, I did not see. At other points along the Niger, —Sansanding, Diafarabé, and Niafounké,—there are administrative posts, branches of several European commercial companies, and Syrian traders. Yet the

character of the valley as a whole is aboriginal and
purely African.

As we approached Kabara, the gay life of the shore
gave place to vast swamps of reeds or marshes. The
river spread out to miles of width. The current ran
swiftly, and the smoothness of the river at times was
heavily disturbed by the strong desert wind. One day
we lost a man overboard. He was a respectable black
from the town of Niafounké. The *René Caillié* at once
cast off its tow and went back and circled the spot
where he had gone down, but nothing could be found
of him, except the prayer rug upon which he had been
kneeling.

Except between Mopti and Kabara, where the river
was high, we ran only daytimes, tying up at night on
some favorable beach. As dusk fell, our crews and passengers would swarm ashore, build numerous fires
along the bank, and gather in talkative and merry
groups before settling down for the night's repose. At
one fire a group of seven or eight blacks would give
themselves up to story telling. One, particularly, had
a long narrative which he was repeatedly called upon
to act out, to the intense delight of the others. At its
climax, his auditors threw themselves on their backs,
kicked their heels in the air and laughed long and
deliriously. They never wearied of having this tale
unfolded anew.

There is genuine fascination in river life, and no life
could be more independent and comfortable than in
a commodious little *chaland*, unless we accept Huckle-
berry Finn's judgment of a Mississippi raft. In the

later weeks of our voyage, the nights were moonlit and, at times, we were under way. Then the scene was really of entrancing beauty. The moon shone through a haze created by the "brume," and gilded and illuminated the broad expanse of water and the vivid green of the low shores. In the cool night air the blacks on the adjacent barges would gather in little groups around pots containing their fires. As the tug pulled the swaying tow from bend to bend of the placid shining flood, we would pick up new lights of little camps and villages. A vast peace and serenity seemed to hold sky and earth, and thoughts and emotions were awakened which only gradually fade from the memory as recollections of this voyage dim and become like a half-remembered dream.

CHAPTER IX

TIMBUKTU owes its importance, clearly enough, to its geographical situation. It is the meeting point of the Sahara and the Sudan. Commerce by river flows toward it from the upper course of the Niger, from Segou, Sansanding, Djenné, and Mopti, and also from the eastward, the region where developed, long before the founding of Timbuktu, the famous empire of Gao. On the desert side it is the focus of long caravan routes, from Morocco, Algeria, and Tripoli. It does not lie on the banks of the river, but a dozen miles north of the main channel, amidst low hillocks of sand, covered with the thorny mimosa scrub, upon which the camels love to feed. The surrounding country is wild and little inhabited, and would be uninteresting except for the mystery which rests upon the Sahara.

The city is really a Saharan achievement, for it was founded by one of the tribes of the Tuareg, the pillaging sons of the desert. As has been stated, these singular folk hold the mid-Saharan mountainous region called the Ahaggar and the smaller and more southerly desert mountains of the Adrar des Iforas, and the Aïr. From these strongholds they have, from time immemorial, carried on their raids against Morocco and Algeria and the oases south of the Atlas, and have ever preyed upon the caravan routes across the Sahara. The valley of the Niger, however, has drawn them from the Sahara *massifs*, and they now live in many thousands, not only in the semi-desert region immediately to the north of the stream, but also in the spacious, arid steppe embraced within the great bend of the Niger, which is known as Hombori. They preserve their nomadic habits, the singular practice of the men of veiling the lower part of the face, their characteristic arms,—sabers, spears and poniards lashed to the forearm,—and, except as now suppressed and restrained by French arms, their innate habit of living by spoliation.

A group of these people, in the eleventh century, at this point, which probably then, as now, contained depressions filled by the extreme flood of the Niger, made a permanent camp. The city was developed by succeeding Sudanese kingdoms and by the Berbers. The name is pronounced by the natives of the region, "Tombúktu" and is said to be a Berber word meaning "the place of *Buktu*," the latter word being here the name of a well, or of an old woman charged with its care. Owing to the great rise and fall of the Niger, the city has really four different ports, utilizable at different seasons of the flood and its recession. The most important of these is the town of Kabara, which can be reached by shallow-draft boats during high water. The approach is a sinuous canal, opened through the swampy ground by one of the rulers of Timbuktu, and it bears his name, El Hadj Omar.

We reached the vicinity of Timbuktu at the height

of the inundation. On all sides the swollen river and the grassy marshes stretched away. The mainland could hardly be seen. On little knolls and elevations, rising above the reeds and water, the semi-nomadic people of the country had crowded for dry footing, with their herds. The evening before reaching Kabara we stopped just after dark at one of these small river settlements. There were no substantial houses, but only circular, bowl-shaped huts of grass and matting. I wandered for half an hour among these curious habitations. Each family group was enclosed by a fence or *zariba*. Little warming fires gleamed everywhere, and about them clustered women and children. From different sides came the sounds of pestle in wooden mortar, the uneasy growls of dogs, the calls and prattle of the groups about the hearths. Every little way was a bunch of cows and calves, tied by a forefoot to stakes or resting peacefully in the mulch of their tether-grounds. It was a primitive life, such as seems to characterize the situation of cattle people everywhere. In the morning a wooden bowl of milk, properly heated by the cook to a reassuring temperatiure, appeared with my early coffee.

We arrived at Kabara, after much difficulty in poling amidst the reedy morasses, about mid-forenoon of the following day. The drawing of the town made by Barth in 1855 shows the community spreading over a considerable hill. But either Barth's eyesight failed him, or the hill has blown away, for only a slight sandy rise of ground bears the uninviting mudhouses and tattered huts which shelter the population of today. Here

A WATER COURSE IN THE SUDAN

TWO WAR VETERANS OF THE VILLAGE OF KANKOMELE

are a small office of the *Navigation,* in charge of a very competent black agent, and a post office and telegraph station in charge of another educated Sudanese. On the outskirts of the town is Fort Aube, garrisoned by a handful of Senegalese riflemen. A mile away rise the tall poles of the radio station, through which one may communicate with Dakar and beyond. Otherwise, the town is purely African. A row of fine shade trees lines the shore, under some of which is a small market, while under others sit groups of idle men, engaged in a game of tit-tat-toe, played with stones on the sand. In the midst of the town is a small mosque, from which the muezzin called each daybreak. Little gardens lie along the river bank. Canoes, bringing forage or fish, come and go. A few dumps of merchandise are piled above the reach of the waters. This is about all presented by the Kabara of today.

The *chef du village* promptly appeared, and, at my request, procured a horse and a guide. I saddled and set off across the rolling, sandy country for Timbuktu. Numbers of goats were pasturing upon the mimosa, little gray doves abounded, and here and there curious birds fluttered amidst the brush. The distance to the city is not far, but in the past it has had an evil reputation, and about midway one passes the site near which Lieutenant Aube and his party were massacred in 1893, and which bears the Berber name of *Our Oumaïra,* which is variously translated, but which seems to mean, "They hear not," referring perhaps to the cries of the waylaid travelers. Near this point, too, Barth noticed a singular tree—"the *talha* tree of the *Weli Salah,* covered with innumerable rags of the superstitious natives, who expected to be generously rewarded by their saint with a new shirt." The tree still stands and is still constantly replenished with tattered votive offerings.

A few miles of further slow travel bring one in sight of the city. On the south side is the French quarter, Fort Bonnier, and well-built houses with cool arcades for the community and the administration, a post-office, a hall of justice, a covered market, and a little plaza around which trees have been planted, which are still small and struggling. At least one commercial company has a good building on this square. Behind are the mud houses of the city, the winding streets and the curious minarets of the famous mosques, which by no means appear as imposing as they are represented to be in the drawing by Barth.

Timbuktu is literally a city builded on the sand, and sand has drifted in, gradually raising the streets, especially on the north side. To enter the houses one must descend a foot or two to the level of the threshold. Sand also has banked up around the famous mosque, Sankoré, and almost threatens to everwhelm it. The city, which at one time extended over a larger area, and may have had 40,000 inhabitants, is today greatly reduced in size and in prosperity and probably has now no more than 4,000 or 5,000 permanent inhabitants. When the French occupied it, it had been reduced by the pillage and exactions of the Tuareg almost to ruin. Today its life is somewhat recovered, but the newer movements of commerce have not permitted it to regain its one-time importance, and it shows little pros-

pect of re-attaining the business and renown which for
centuries distinguished it.

The houses, however, are well built and quite interesting. They are entered by ornamental doorways, the
wooden frame being carved with attractive patterns
and doors studded with great nail-heads. A second
story usually covers the front part of the building,
leaving the rear to form a spacious flat roof or terrace.
Here and there, in open spaces, are large dome-like
ovens, and the central market is a place of animation,
where mingle the strangest types, blends of the many
breeds which have added their character to the con-
fused population of the city.

Timbuktu was at one time a noted center of the
slave trade and, until the French occupation, manacled
captives were brought here from many directions, and
formed the dolorous caravans which were taken up the
Niger or, at prodigious hardship and loss of life, were
forced across the Sahara to supply the slave demand
of Marrakech or of Tripoli.

Today, the active commerce of the city seems to
rest upon the salt trade with the desert mines of
Taodéni, which is one of the most remarkable pieces
of commerce to be found anywhere. Almost due north
of Timbuktu, about midway in the crossing to Southern Morocco and *en plein Sahara*, are famous deposits of hard crystalline salt, which lie in a succession
of separate strata only a few meters below the sand.
Here is quarried the salt which, in large slabs or little
fragments, passes from hand to hand over an enormous
area of the Sudan. Hundreds of miles south and east

of Timbuktu, one meets little groups of negro traders, their asses laden with this highly prized product of the mines of Taodéni. The mines are properties of the Moors and under the jurisdiction of a Moorish kadi. They are worked by slaves. The enterprise of bringing the salt to the Niger is a Moorish undertaking, although based on Timbuktu. Twice a year a caravan is formed to cross the desert, and bring back to the city the semi-annual supply. The desert north and east of Timbuktu, being generally covered with sparse thorn bushes, is a famous breeding and pasture ground for the camel, and here the animals are raised and recruited.

Few white men, I gather, have ever seen Taodéni. It was located with exactness by René Caillié on his return from Timbuktu across the Sahara. The caravan which Dr. Oskar Lenz accompanied in 1880 passed around Taodéni without approaching the mines or the town. In 1906 the famous organizer of the meharistes, General Laperrine, pushed across from the oasis region of Touat to the northeast, and reached Taodéni, where, by a pre-concerted arrangement, he was met by a similar military exploring party coming north from Araoan. I know of but one other European who has visited these salt mines.

One moonlit evening, while at Kabara, I was sitting smoking on the shore, when I was approached by an old and venerable Frenchman with the long white beard of a patriarch, who courteously entered into conversation and, declining a chair, seated himself cross-legged in Arab fashion on the sand. He began to talk

QUARANTINE STATION AGAINST TYPHUS ABOVE SEGOU

TYPES OF SUDANESE WOMEN OF THE NIGER

SUDANESE CATTLE ON THE NIGER WITH THEIR FULA HERDSMEN

to me of Timbuktu and the Sahara. For two hours he
held me spellbound. Quickly it became apparent that
here was no ordinary adventurer, but a learned man
with a profound knowledge of the Sudan, a scholar in
the legal and religious systems which the religion of
Mohammed has spread over this part of Africa. Later
I learned that this gentleman was M. Dupuis, better
known locally by his title of "Yakouba," whose writings I had seen, and something of whose singular history had been communicated to me. Many years ago
he went to Africa, a priest in the famous missionary
crusading order of "The White Fathers," (les Pères
Blancs), founded by Cardinal Lavigerie as a revived
form of militant Christianity, dedicated to the suppression of the slave trade, and to opposition to the spread
of Islam. Love of women, and other disturbing influences of the African continent, are said to have led
this man to renounce his vows and separate himself
from the priesthood and from his order. For thirty-
three years he has lived in Timbuktu, the head of a
considerable patriarchal family, and a person of much
influence among the inhabitants of the region. He saw
the city as it was when Joffre occupied it, ruined and
pillaged by the Tuareg. He saw the slave-market and
its captives, their legs bloody under their chains. So
far as a white man may, he has probably penetrated
the barrier that bars the mind and emotions of one
race from the exact apprehension of another.

In 1907 M. Dupuis accompanied the salt caravan
to Taodéni, and what I set down here now about this
enterprise is gathered from his conversation. The route

taken is first from Timbuktu to the oasis of Araoan,
and thence directly northward eleven days of travel
and five hundred kilometers of desert without a drop
of water or a spear of food for the animals. The
camels are carefully trained for this hard test, their
preparation including, at first, water once in four
days, then in six, then in eight, and, finally, once
in ten. There is no pasture for them throughout the
route, which lies across a shrubless, gravelly waste.
There is water at two points, Felfal and Bir Ounan,
but the supply is trivial, and does not even suffice for
the men of the expedition. At Taodéni the halt is brief,
two or three days, during which the camels are watered
from brackish wells; then the straight, hard push
back to Araoan. Thus, there is a period of twenty-
five days of travel in which the camels go entirely without food, and have only one drink of water. The animals reach Timbuktu emaciated and exhausted, and
are turned out for pasturage and recuperation for a
period of six months before being called upon again
for further service.

The ordeal for the men is scarcely less severe. The
travel is from dawn to dusk. The water ration is three
litres a day to a man, which, in the dry atmosphere of
the desert, probably leaves him in constant thirst. A
meal is taken once a day in the evening and consists of
a small bowl of *dhurra* or porridge, and, as Dupuis
phrased it, "the belt is tightened each day." Every two
hours the caravan, which marches under a species of
military discipline, halts for ten minutes. Water for
the men is carried in skins holding about forty litres

each. Of these, one camel can carry four, amounting to 160 litres, or a drinking supply for four men for eleven days.

Taodéni is built within a *kasbah* or mud fortress, perhaps 250 meters square. There are two wells within the walls. All food is brought from Timbuktu. The mining is done by slaves brought from Timbuktu, and returned to that city for recuperation after a period of their arduous labor. The salt lies in a number of strata, only a few meters beneath the sand, and in the upper layers are found the fossil remains of the hippopotamus, the elephant and other African mammalia. Government and justice are in the hands of the Moorish kadi, already mentioned. From Taodéni the route leads by way of Tendouf to the Draa in southern Morocco and thence to Mogador or to Marrakech.

The road over which slaves were (and still are), transported to Morocco takes a circuitous route to the eastward from Araoan in the following stages: Timbuktu to Bou Djebeha,—eight days over brushy country in which the animals find both water and pasture; then from Bou Djebeha to the wells of El Mihraheti,—two days, where there is some of the desert bunch grass, called by the Arabs *alfa*, on which the camels feed; thence to In Chaig,—three days; thence to El Guettara,—four days; and thence to the Wadi Telig,—two days, where there are numerous wells, and whence it is only a short distance to Taodéni.

Besides the foods already mentioned, the camel pastures on a little bunch grass, perhaps ten inches high, which the Arabs call *hadh*, but the mimosa, because of its hardihood, its relative abundance, and the singular taste the camel has for its twigs and formidable spines, must be reckoned the main support of the Saharan camels.

The salt is quarried in large bars or blocks which formerly sold for five francs, and now bring forty-five. Because of its fine crystalline quality, its beautiful appearance, its resistance to moisture, and probably other traditional qualities, it is prized in the Sudan by millions of people above the salt from any other source. Foreign salt from Spain or elsewhere is now coming in down the Niger to take its place, and I saw very active trade in this article in the market at Mopti. But the Taodéni commerce, which alone appears to sustain the city of Timbuktu, continues to represent a considerable trade. The semi-annual caravan comprises four to five thousand camels. I understood M. Dupuis, however, to say that the enterprise has greatly declined, and that the caravan which he accompanied in 1907 embraced at least 15,000 camels, and the corresponding number of men, was probably one to each five animals, or 3,000 persons. To conduct such a force in an organized, disciplined way, guarding the endurance of men and beasts, protecting the frugal issue of water and food, for a thousand kilometers, across the worst section of the Sahara must, I think, be considered an exercise of command of no mean power, involving training, coöperation, and subordination of a high character.

Immediately on the north side of Timbuktu stands a walled fort built by Joffre to protect the city on the desert side, and beyond this fort is a sandy region called the *Abaradian,* or camel suburb, where the camels are discharged of their burdens, and where, at one side, are clustered a great number of low, squalid huts occupied by the population which attends upon the camel caravans, and which seems to belong to a lower caste than the merchants and house dwellers of Timbuktu.

Wandering across this space one morning, I came upon a detachment of meharistes, composed of a few French *sous-officiers,* barefooted, and burned almost to the brown of the Berber, and numbers of the desert tribesmen, who had been incorporated as troopers in this remarkable service. These were the wildest looking men I have ever seen. Some of them were swathed in turbans and face cloths up to the eyes. Their arms, skins, and accoutrements hung along the camel's sides and under his belly. They had been upon some hard service and were about to move out into the pasture-grounds for recuperation of man and beast. A dead camel lay here and there, the tenderloin of the abandoned creature cut away, probably for food.

An officer in command of the fort hospitably took me into his quarters, and showed me several treasures salvaged from the desert, including very interesting implements of the Polished Stone Age. Like his companions, he was as hard and brown as old rawhide, though still young. The photograph of a young French lady stood on his desk, the only visible souvenir of the country which had sent him into this service. "It's a hard life, I suppose," I remarked, but after the manner of his kind who have gained an attachment for the mystery, the freedom, the open air of this vast desert space, he would not admit it. "One becomes accustomed," was all he would say. His attitude is typical of these Frenchmen, separated for such long periods of service from the beautiful country which is their home, but steadfast, without disposition to criticize or admit ground of complaint for the task in which they are engaged.

At Timbuktu I was entertained by the commandant of the city and region, Major Fauché, and by his wife, who had recently joined him. They occupied a good, spacious adobe building, surrounded by double galleries, which Madame Fauché had made attractive with souvenirs of her husband's life, and with adornments lent by the decorative arts of the desert and the Sudan peoples. Major Fauché has spent a lifetime in this service, broken only by four years on the French front during the war. He has a wound stripe for each of those years. He seems devoted to the desert, and to the hard conditions that surround his duty. Glancing about the court and quarters transformed by the art of Madame into a charming French ménage, he observed, "Since the beginning of my service this is the first house that I have ever occupied, and now that I have a house I have to go outdoors to sleep."

The military force at Timbuktu, considering the strategic importance of the place, seems small—a battalion of the *Tirailleurs,* and detachments of meharistes who occupy distant isolated posts in the desert and patrol its routes. But between Kabara

and Timbuktu a spacious landing place is being
cleared and leveled in the sand, and an aviation
port established,—one of ten in the Sudan,—and it is
upon airplanes that the French will tend to depend in
their measures to impress and control the rebellious
spirit of the Sahara and Sudan. None the less, Timbuktu is probably open to a raid from the same quarter from which it has been conquered in the past,
namely, southern Morocco. In October, 1923, such a
razzia occurred. A party of Berbers crossed the Sahara,
hung around the vicinity for a time in the guise of
traders, then swooped upon a mehariste detachment
making camp and destroyed it. They secured a considerable booty of arms, camels and captives, and got
away across the desert. But the rear guard of the party
was overtaken by a French punitive force, filling their
water bags preparatory to their return, on the shores
of Lake Faguibine. The incident suggests that French
control of Morocco south of the Atlas, now exercised
through support of *"les Grands Kaids,"* is not wholly
satisfactory from the standpoint of the protection of
the Sudan.

The religious prestige and wide spiritual influence
of Timbuktu are represented in its three mosques and
its *médersa,* or university. These mosques are probably among the most famous in Africa. The largest of
them, called the Djingeri Ber, is known to have been
built about 600 years ago. The two others are the
mosque of the Sankoré, said to have been founded
through the piety of a woman, and the shrine of Sidi
Yahiá. It was the Sankoré that sheltered the long suc-

cession of religious teachers and scholars who gave Timbuktu its academic fame. In this mosque was produced the *opus magnum* of negro Africa, the famous *El Tarikh es Sudan.* This work was translated from the Arabic by Professor Houdas and published at Paris. It ranks as an authentic and quite priceless history of the Niger Valley and the empires which flourished within it. But a large portion of the Tarikh and, not the least interesting, is that devoted to the lives and works of the scholars and holy persons of the Sankoré. A member myself of an academic circle, on reading the encomiums of these worthy men, I am moved to wonder whether a future historian may ever have so much to say in homage of an American company of scholars.

An effort is being made by the French to perpetuate Timbuktu as a center of both Arabic and French instruction. The ancient Médersa of Djenné has been moved to Timbuktu, and a neat little edifice constructed for the accommodation of classes. Here I found half a dozen alert, hospitable scholars, all blacks, with classes of young Sudanese being taught in both French and Arabic, and a small but interesting library comprising famous books in both languages. However it may be today or in the future, the Sudanese retain their reverence for the learning and sanctity of the city, and Du Bois quotes a Sudanese proverb: "Salt comes from the north, gold from the south, and silver from the country of the white man; but the word of God and the treasures of wisdom can only be found at Timbuktu."

A BAKE OVEN AT A STREET CORNER IN TIMBUKTU

A TYPICAL DWELLING IN TIMBUKTU

A BULLOCK ENTERING MOPTI LADEN WITH BAGS OF TRADE SALT

The limits of the city have become much restricted. There are suburbs, apparently once peopled, now covered by sand. Barth thought Timbuktu in his time had 13,000 settled inhabitants and claims to have counted the clay houses and found them to be about 980. But the resident population today cannot exceed 4,000 or 5,000, and a large portion of it is being drawn away for labor in the cotton enterprise further up the Niger at Diré, of which some mention will be made further on. The real importance of the locality is strategic. If not firmly held as it is by the French, it would speedily again become a rendezvous of the predatory Tuareg and Moors. Held as it is, it is the military key to the routes across the Sahara and to the domination of the *boucle* of the Niger. The only surprise is that it can be securely held by so small a force of armed men. The Tuareg, however, I was assured by Commandant Fauché, are thoroughly subdued. The only menace is in the combative and raiding instinct of the South Atlas Berbers.

CHAPTER X

ON reaching Mopti on my return from Timbuktu, I at once made preparations to set out on the travel across the Sudan as far as Ouagadougou. It was a very simple matter. The administrateur, a sunburned, robust French official, energetic in every word and movement, promptly gave orders to a native orderly to supply me with two horses, two horse boys and ten porters. Later, I received a document from the "bureau" giving the names of these men and the conditions of their service and employment. They were to accompany me as far as Bandiagara. The next morning, at a satisfactorily early hour, horses and men were on hand.

The horse of the Sudan is a small, well shaped animal, white, bay, sorrel, black, doubtless derived from the Arab, but lacking the fine muzzle and small pointed ears of his forebear. He has a good disposition, and is usually well broken, the best of them to a rack or to a pace. The saddle equipment is serviceable, highly ornamented, and strikingly similar to that which the Spaniard generalized in Mexico, whence it was carried to the Western United States. There is the same large pommel and high cantle, the decorated leather, the heavy bit, with the high, cruel "port" of the "Spanish", or "Breed" bit, the same useful and ornamental trappings for keeping the horse's head and flanks free from flies. The best horse I saw in the Sudan was a fine white stallion, the property of a *Hausa* cattle trader from Kano in British northern Nigeria, whose name was Amul Assa. This horse, while no more than 149 centimeters in height (57 inches), was powerful, spirited and beautifully gaited. I had expected to buy my horses, but it takes time to negotiate a good horse trade, and I found it so easy to rent passable animals that I decided not to embarrass myself with the cares of possession. The horse-boys were Fulas and were considered indispensable for the proper care of the animals.

The porters on the several stages to Ouagadougou were the most remarkable burden bearers I have ever encountered. Their necks and shoulders were extraordinarily developed, and their physiques, generally, robust and vigorous. The average weight of their loads was about 30 kilos. With such burdens balanced on their heads, they moved off at a long swinging walk that quite uniformly covered five kilometers an hour. One forenoon, starting two hours before daylight, with a brief halt, during which they consumed a quantity of sour milk mixed with *kouskous,* they marched 25 miles. On another day, in two stages, the last running well into the evening, they actually went 55 kilometers or approximately 35 miles. These are very long marches for loaded men, and only possible to men of special vigor, cheerfulness, and courage.

The marching was not always easy. The route fre-

quently was across light, sandy soil. Some of the men
wore a primitive leather sandal, but others were barefooted. The soles of their feet were encrusted with
a covering of horny callous skin, surpassing anything
I have ever seen. But this dry dead skin cracked fear-
fully, particularly under the toes and across the sole
of the foot. I followed the practice of bathing these
sore spots with an antiseptic solution or sponging them
with iodine, softening the area somewhat with an oxide
ointment, and then protecting the foot with broad
strips of surgeon's plaster. These remedies seemed to
give the men relief, and they became anxious to have
them applied, and were most grateful for their provision. I cannot speak too highly of the temper and disposition of these simple men. In no part of the world
have I found the problem of handling men so easy; nor
met with such implicit willingness to take orders and
carry out the mission cheerfully. I think I should add,
in conclusion, that the pay of these men amounted to
about seven cents a day in American exchange.

We left Mopti by a well-built, tree-lined causeway,
which extends for several kilometers across the swampy
ground, and separates the shore of the river from the
higher dry land of the interior. Then, for several days,
the route lay through low hills, and along timbered
water courses in a country, sparsely settled but abound-
ing in game. In the roughest part of this hilly region,
not very far from Mopti, I was assured by both
Frenchmen and natives that there are lions, but I
heard no sounds more formidable than the shrill cry,

THE GREAT MOSQUE (DJINGERÉ BER) AT TIMBUKTU

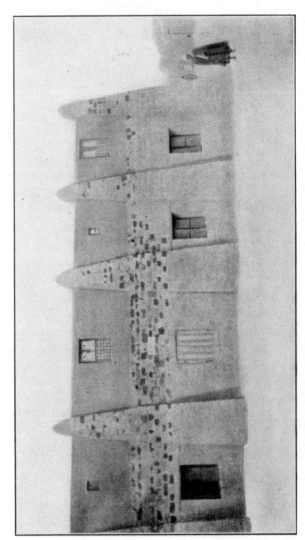

A BUILDING OF THE NEWLY ORGANIZED UNIVERSITY OR MEDERSA AT TIMBUKTU

in the hours before dawn, of the little jackal, or
kungúlu, as he is known to the natives. The land is
too populated for the great types of African fauna.
South of Bandiagara, the country rises gradually in
slopes and hills that end precipitously in an abrupt
cliff that extends northeasterly and southwesterly for
hundreds of miles and terminates in the desert of
Hombori south of the great bend of the Niger. This
cliff is spoken of as *La Falaise de Bandiagara.* There
must have occurred a sharp faulting, which gave rise
to this striking cliff, which forms the watershed between the river systems of the Niger and of the Volta.
The precipice is only a few hundred feet high, but is
very imposing. It is very steep, and is a considerable
obstacle to roads or trails. It has weathered in such
a manner as to overhang, and leave against the foot
of the cliff a talus of broken rock. Under this overhang, the Habé people have built cliff villages, which
strikingly resemble the cliff dwellings of Southwestern
United States. Nearest to the foot of the talus is the
line of houses and stout protective walls. Above these
rise tall, rectangular granaries, frequently decorated
with odd designs. Still higher up, and reached by
ladders against the cliff, are mud and straw beehives
of this honey-loving people. In the broad plain at the
foot of the cliff lie millet fields and wells. There seems
to be a disposition, now, for the Habés to build their
homes on this level ground, but this must be due to
the increased sense of security due to French rule,
for they always told me that their resort to their cliff

dwellings was for protection against enemies, especially
the Fula.

One of the most singular of these Habé settlements
—I should say "Kado settlements", because Kado is
the singular form while Habé (or Ábé) is plural,—is
the village of Fiko (or Piko), between Mopti and
Bandiagara. It is built on a rock mesa, like the Indian
village of Moki. The path ascends up the side of the
rock, and at one or two places is aided by a ladder
formed of a heavy log. At one point the trail passes
through a cave. The houses are built partly of stone.
There were many in an abandoned state. According to
the chief, the village now has only about forty people,
but the evidence is unmistakable that this was at one
time the citadel of a persecuted race.

South and east of the Falaise the plain extends for
hundreds of miles, unbroken by any elevation of importance, until far to the south one encounters the
Kong Mountains. Everywhere, the light, reddish soil
is covered with brush, which the French call *la brousse*,
and which would seem to correspond to the English use
of the word "bush". Tall fine trees rise here and there
above this "chapparal", but the forest is a scattered
one except along the watercourses, which are crossed
perhaps once in fifty miles. On the north, this bush
thins out into what is called the "Sahel", an intermediate zone between the Sahara and the Sudan. On
the south the bush increases in density until it merges
in the tropical forest.

This character of country I judge to be typical of
the best portions of the Sudan and is, in general, quite

like that of Northern Nigeria. While the soil seems light, there is sufficient rainfall in the summer to support not only the brush, but luxuriant grass, and, except in seasons of drought, to assure good crops of the two staples of native life, the millet and the yam.

The population is considerable, and increases in numbers as one enters the Mossi territory, north of Ouahigouya. In fact, every few miles one comes out of the brush into clearings covered with stubble fields and finds little villages, which in some cases expand into the proportions of large towns. The character of these communities varies appreciably as one passes from the Niger watershed, where the influence of Islam prevails, into the countries of pagan or fetishist tribes. In the former, the plan and architecture of the towns have the character of those of the Niger banks. There are rectangular terraced houses of mud. Winding streets lead to little squares shaded with fine trees, where the *djoulas* or traveling merchant class spread their wares—cloth, salt and kola nuts. Flesh, milk, and meal are offered for sale by the people of the town. Picturesque groups are always chatting and bargaining, while little asses with empty panniers nibble at dry corn husks, or at the debris of the square. There is usually a deep well in these little plazas, and at one corner a dark smithy, where men of the iron-working caste beat out on stone anvils the rude, elongated hoes, knives, weapons and other implements of daily life.

In the villages near the Niger there is always a mosque which, further south, is supplanted by singular buildings of differing type, that appear to be lodges for fetish worship or for social reunion. These last structures are low, built partly of posts and planks, and partly of stone. Set up around them are heavy thick planks on which a woman's figure is over and over again carved in high relief or indicated by conventionalized shapes of mammæ. In all these villages the granaries are important. They are built of mud, are square and tall, and set up from the ground. The corn is ground by the women on stone mills like the *metates* of Mexico or the Southwest, and in one little village, called Koro, I saw a sort of communal mill, a circular mud platform sixteen feet across between the outer edges, on which were set no less than fifteen grinding stones.

There was always considerable of interest in the life of these little towns, particularly toward evening. From my camp on the outskirts, it was entertaining to watch sunset pass, and the line of sky become brilliant with gorgeous colors. Silhouetted against the horizon line would be pointed, thatched roofs, the tops of granaries, and behind these the beautiful tracery of thin-foliaged trees. At a little distance the Mohammedan men of my party would be engaged in vociferous prayer, first performing the prescribed ablutions, not with water but with sand, rubbing the palms with a little earth and touching the face and forehead, then kneeling, standing, prostrating themselves with brow to the ground. From the brush would come winding the lines of lowing cattle, and each well would be a scene of great exertion. A group of twenty-five or thirty men would engage in drawing the water with leather buckets and long rawhide lines. One night, at the village of Pel Maounde, I measured these "well ropes", and found that it took 120 feet to reach the water. The process of watering the herd goes on for two or three hours, the animals gradually moving off and lying down for rest in the village square or courtyard.

There was something picturesque and moving about these evening scenes,—the level millet-fields slowly disappearing in the shadows, the tall, park-like trees, amidst them the contorted shapes of the *baobab*, the soft noise of a flute arising above the babble of the village, stars pricking out through the gray skies,—a sense of peace and contentment, mingled with an atmosphere of mystery and of human tragedy,—my men, meanwhile, clustering hungrily around their bowls of porridge and then rolling up in their light cotton coverings for rest upon the hard ground.

The French have had constructed along this main route a succession of lodges for European travelers, which they call *campements*. These consist of several well built mud huts, with pointed, thatched roofs, two of them being invariably reserved for Europeans. The others are kitchens, stables, and lodgings for the men. Usually a mud wall surrounds the whole enclosure, and fine thorn trees often shade the camp. There are always stout picket pins driven into the ground at the corners of the yard, for the tethering of horses.

It was usually at such bungalows that my party camped. Invariably our arrival was immediately followed by the appearance of the village chief, some-

times with a little group of attendants, who came to
find out what was wanted, and who instantly trans-
mitted my requests for water, fuel, forage, and porridge for the men, into orders that were accomplished
as fast as ready hands could comply. The prices for
these services were nominal, and payment always
evoked appreciative recognition. The staple food for
the men of my party was a kind of mush called *túo*,
made of ground millet-seed and flavored with a kind
of brown, thin sauce, the exact composition of which
I never mastered. But a great deal depended on this
sauce and its flavor, and it was always tested by my
men before it was accepted as satisfactory. The porridge
took several hours to prepare, and was usually brought
into camp, after what seemed a long period of waiting,
by a little column of children with the large wooden
bowls on their curly heads. It was upon this porridge,
served twice a day, at noon and at night, that my
men depended, and with it they were content, although
grateful for any additions to the ration such as venison, fowl, mutton, and especially sour milk, purchased
from time to time from Fula women. There may be
some virtue in the sour quality of the milk drunk, and
in this matter the African may have anticipated the
discoveries of Metchnikoff. At any rate the Sudanese
seem to prefer milk in this condition.

The whole process of travel has, in some way, been
admirably systematized. I never had reason for complaint at delay in the services rendered by these villages, and their head men. And one further thing I
wish to record. In all the weeks of this experience I

never lost a single article through pilfering, not because I am particularly careful of property, for I am
not, but because the people of these villages and my
own men were apparently highly regardful of the
sanctity of property, and under no impulse wrongfully
to appropriate it for themselves.

We usually commenced our march very early in the
day, quite two hours before dawn. I inaugurated this
Spartan practice myself, but the African is imitative, and
my cook Anadí promptly took upon himself the responsibility of routing me out in the middle of the night.
I would hear his voice at an unexpectedly early hour,
"*Mon Colonel, mon Colonel*", (usually a little louder
with each repetition), "*le premier cocq à chanté!*".
After that there was nothing to do but get up, and
sure enough, in some remote village would be heard
some misguided fowl caroling the interval before the
coming of dawn. My cook always had ready for me
a measure of hot coffee, packs were quickly formed,
horses saddled, and in a little interval of time we would
be moving easily through the brush, only half-sensitive
to the broad landscape about us.

There is something mysterious in the brush at this
hour of the night, before game begins to stir. We would
pass little collections of huts, their inmates still sleeping, with fires extinguished. Occasionally in the darkness the trail would be lost. Gradually dawn would
come, with a vast irradiation of the sky, and then, at
the next stop, the Mohammedan men in my party,
(and there were always a few), would make haste to
spread their rugs or prayer skins and give voice to

that wild, exultant summoning of men to arise and praise God, with which the day is welcomed.

Our stops in the middle of the day usually lasted for several hours, while food was prepared in the near-by villages, and my men slept off the morning's fatigue. My cook would busy himself with the boiling of water and the preparation of a substantial noon meal, while I cleaned guns, fussed with equipment, and sometimes entertained for a period the village chieftain and his attendants, who would come out with ceremony to salute me. It was noticeable, however, that these men, respects having been paid, and orders for our accommodation issued, never hung about or molested one with their attentions. Unless invited to stay and sit, they promptly departed, having conducted themselves with dignity and a native courtesy that were very pleasing.

I had one man in my party, after leaving Bandiagara, whom I recall with special pleasure. His name was Barka, and he was a Toucouleur, a member of that warlike tribe which has played a large part in the military history of the Sudan. Barka was a man of impressive size and stature, 177 centimeters tall. He had served for six years in the French army and its discipline and experience had made him grave and formal, and at the same time loyal and responsive. He was a man of superior mind and character. He retained from his army experience a little memory of the French language. Why he should have been found in a company of porters or burden bearers, I never could decide, unless it was that he shared the usual fortune of the ex-soldier, and was poor. This man was of assistance to me always, for his knowledge of the country was extensive and accurate, and his influence among the men authoritative. He was as fine a trained companion as a white man could have in traversing regions of Africa in which he was inexperienced and alone. I parted from this man with a sense of real regret, and with an esteem for him which had risen with each day of his service. He was a Mohammedan. In spite of his poverty, he dressed carefully in the long white robe which the Mohammedan Sudanese· wear, and which has a direct relation to their self-respect and their pride of bearing. He was very methodical in his devotions, usually retiring a little from the company to a spot, where he would be undisturbed, but where his acts of devotion could be widely observed and have their appropriate influence upon the pagan mind.

During this period of travel, while I usually wore a belt carrying a Colt's revolver, I believe that the exhibition or possession of arms was really unnecessary. French occupation has brought peace and order to all this region. It is hard to believe that only a few years ago it was continually being devastated by warfare, pillage, slavery, and the most horrible forms of oppression and cruelty. Nothing is more impressive about French authority in this land than the way in which they have made conditions just, livable, and humane.

As we passed out of the region inhabited by the village-dwelling Habés and the nomadic, cattle-raising Fula, and entered the country of the Mossi, a change

occurred both in the physical type of the race and in
the character of the villages, architecture, and arts
of life. This change is perhaps first noticed at Ouahigouya, a very large community in the midst of a great
brushy plain, which is the post of a *cercle,* the unit

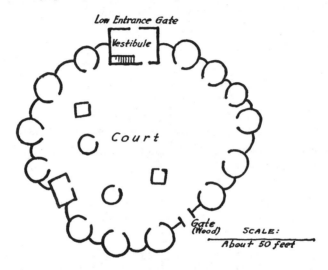

GROUND PLAN OF COMPOUND OR KRAAL OF
MOSSI CHIEF (NABA) AT OUAHIGOUYA

of French administration. The town is divided into
many communal groups, each consisting of a cluster
of family establishments. These latter are formed by
a series of round huts, set in a circle, with high con-
cave walls binding the huts together. The accompanying plan, which represents, in a general way, the arrangement of the compound of a chieftain, may make
clearer this plan of domicile. This particular chief's

compound was entered through a large rectangular mud building with a flat roof, which appeared to be a vestibule. The building was whitewashed and rather impressive. The chief, or *nabá*, was a large, heavy man, with a face somewhat clouded by sensuality and the exercise of power. He came to greet me with a dozen people in his retinue, including a young man who spoke French quite clearly, which he told me he had learned in the local school.

The formalities practiced by such a Mossi chieftain on approaching a European are elaborate. He is invariably attended by a number of men who seem to be his staff and councillors, and also by several young pages called *soroné* who are of a peculiar character. They are selected at about the age of eighteen for intelligence and comeliness, and during the period of their service in this capacity must lead a strictly chaste life. They dress themselves very foppishly, and wear their hair in a highly elaborate coxcomb along the crown of the head from brow to nape of neck. They clothe themselves in long flowing gowns and are so effeminate in appearance and behavior that, when I saw the first such party, I was puzzled as to whether they were men or women.

When such a chief and his retainers approach, they all squat down and, as a sign of greeting and of respect, beat the earth gently with the backs of their hands. The pages, meanwhile, snap the fingers against the palms, making a sharp clacking noise. There is usually a flutist or a harpist in the party, who intermittently produces subdued strains of music. One can hardly fail to be interested, not to say gratified, by such testimony of good breeding and politeness. These marks of ceremony and esteem find their culmination in the court of the Great King of the Mossi, the Moro Nabá, at Ouagadougou.

The Mossi nation numbers approximately a million souls. For at least 800 years it has had an established political organization centering in the Great King, and has been both warlike and set upon. Probably a considerable proportion of the slaves rendezvoused in the valley of the Niger were gathered by raids upon the Mossi, and the Mossi at times carried their own forays to such a point as to seize and occupy Timbuktu. They are pagans or fetishists, and long served as a barrier against the southward penetration of Mohammedanism, but it seemed to me that, now that peace has been established between them and the tribes of the north, Mohammedanism is penetrating among them. In the towns south of Ouahigouya, at least, there were almost invariably mosques, and outside the boundaries of these settlements, at evening time, there was always a group of impressively gowned men, facing toward Mecca, in prayer.

Near the Mossi town of Lay, I observed a rather singular burial place which they told me was called "yawgo". There were about 100 interments, and these were made in great jars called "singga". The remains are either placed in these jars and covered over with earth or buried underneath them. There was a hole broken in each urn. The chief informed me that only important people are buried in this way.

The French officials, I believe, rightly place considerable importance upon this powerful Mossi people, and they have been highly successful in their relations with them. The governor of the colony of the Haute Volta told me that the Moro Nabá was a man of exceptional character and loyalty. The position has been hereditary in his family for 800 years, and there is an established tradition that the Moro Nabá never leaves the capital of Ouagadougou. The present king, however, has a son whom he has consented to have sent for study to Tunisia where the climate is considered favorable. I saw two of his daughters in attendance at the school for girls located in this French post, one of whom desires to be trained as a nurse or *sage femme*. The father of the present ruler accepted French authority, and the son has been especially devoted in his allegiance. While under the French system administrative authority is entirely vested in the governor, the Moro Nabá is consulted, and his political and religious influence utilized. He has a chief minister and several other ministers in charge of agriculture, trade, stock raising, and war. The chiefs of the district who have oversight over the chiefs of villages pay to the Moro Nabá a devotion cultivated by centuries of obedience, and consider him in authority only second to the French commander.

Ouagadougou has been a French post for a good many years. Trees planted at the founding of the station, now overhang the streets and are filled with bright and noisy birds. There are the bureau of the cercle, the military post, several trading houses, comfortable

residences each occupying a full block, a mission of
the White Fathers, and to the east of the old town
a new group of government buildings, erected since
the Haute Volta became a separate colony. These
buildings include the residence of the governor and
the branches of administration.

There is here an interesting native hospital in charge
of a devoted physician. This hospital had only been
open a few months, but the doctor was fully occupied
with cases, and there were about a hundred out-
patients daily applying for relief. The buildings were
of mud or adobe, grouped on a pavilion plan and
divided into wards. One of these wards was for ma-
ternity cases, which, in spite of anticipations to the
contrary, was being well patronized. The doctor had
as assistants a young native who had been medically
trained, and a mid-wife or *sage femme* who was a
young woman of mixed French and black parentage.
The doctor stated that there was little intestinal in-
fection in that colony, but he was having a good many
pulmonary as well as malarial cases. Tropical ulcers
he was successfully treating by fumigating them with
iodoform.

There is one curious affliction which besets the native especially during the wet season, from June to
December. It is the Guinea-worm which finds lodg-
ment under the skin of the limbs, and grows within
the leg to the proportions of an angleworm. These
worms have to be extricated with care lest they be
broken off in the process. The native digs around in
the ulcer formed by his little enemy, and captures it

by the tail. This tail he then fastens to a small stick which he leaves dangling from his leg. Each day the body of the worm is wound up a little more tightly over the stick until it is gradually withdrawn from the wound.

Ouagadougou is a center also in the French plan of instruction. This plan provides primary or village schools, of which there are sixteen in the colony of Haute Volta, with native teachers who have secured their education at Dakar, a regional school giving three years of instruction, and a superior school giving two. Graduates of this last school are selected on a competitive basis to complete their education at Dakar. Instruction is entirely free, and for the superior school there is a home and refectory. The object of these schools is, primarily, to train office assistants, the postal clerks, telegraph operators, mechanics, chauffeurs and nurses. School gardens are attached to these schools, and are generally excellent. In them are raised all kinds of vegetables, and also bananas, papayas, and pineapples. A few are experimenting with lemon trees and grape-vines.

The route from Ouagadougou to the Côte d'Ivoire proceeds southwesterly across a country that gradually becomes more thickly forested with shrubs and trees. The upper waters of the Volta Noire are crossed by a ferry near the post of Boromo. In the dry season it is a stream of only about a hundred feet in width, but in the rainy season it is a great current, five hundred to six hundred meters wide. The tropical forest spreads northward along the course of such streams, and with the forest comes the tse tse fly—the transmitter of the sleeping sickness. There was a region here of about thirty kilometers breadth apparently without inhabitants, a sort of "no man's land", between the Mossi and the tribes to the west and south.

The Bobos whose villages presently appeared are apparently a numerous African tribe, but of a lower order of intelligence and culture than the Mossi. The stark nakedness attributed to Africa begins to show itself among these people. The clothing and adornment of the women are limited to smooth shaving of the head, a stone or glass pin which protrudes from a hole punctured in the lower lip, a belt and little aprons made of fresh plaited leaves about the size of the two hands. The lives of the Bobos are obviously poverty-stricken, though their markets are thronged. The center of their administration is Bobo Djoulasso. The post here is an attractive one. Fine gardens surround the residence. The streets are shaded by kapok trees with their brilliant blossoms, and by mangos. The administrative personnel here forms quite a little colony. There are the administrateur and his wife, an assistant administrateur, a captain of troops, an inspector, a chief of postal service. A garage is maintained, and during the dry season a limited automobile service is furnished from this point. The natives are "fetishists" or pagans, but even in this circle, an occasional mosque was seen, supported, I suppose, by the nomadic Fulas or by the wandering tradesmen, "djoulas", from the valley of the Niger and Senegambia.

HABE VILLAGE (KANKOMELE) UNDER THE CLIFF OF BANDIAGARA

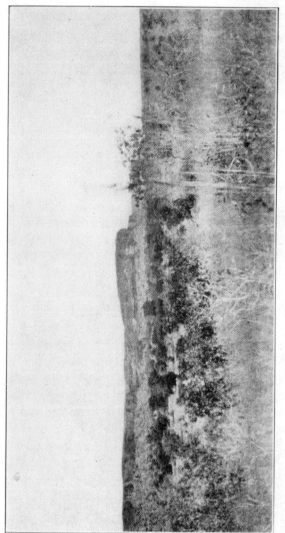

THE FALAISE OR CLIFF OF BANDIAGARA

This is the country explored successfully, for the first time, by Captain L. G. Binger, who cleared up the uncertainties of this region, more than thirty years ago, by a long wandering between the Niger and the Gulf of Guinea. It was Binger's travel which exploded the myth of the Kong mountains, the first notice of which was brought to Europe by Park, who had received a false report of their impassability. It was supposed that they formed a barrier to communication between the tropical forest and the Sudan. As a matter of fact the Kong mountains are only a line of low hills, but they are precipitous on the south side, and are singularly eroded into grotesque buttes and wild ravines.

Passing this natural boundary line, one leaves behind the Sudan, its red level plains, its sparse scrub, its clear atmosphere, and begins to enter the region of heavier forestation. Here, with the approach of the rainy season, the sky became overcast and rent with thunderstorms, and the air was humid and oppressive. It was towards sunset of such a day that I reached the little post of Darakolondougou. Here I was welcomed by the chief of the subdivision—a hearty, likable officer, who was a native of the Hautes Pyrennées, and had passed his life in the service. With him, as a visitor, was a fellow official—a young man of delicate face and refined manners, who was a graduate of the University of Toulouse. A "courrier" had arrived two days before, and the broad table in the garden was piled with French newspapers and magazines. We sat in the dusk while dinner was being prepared, and they gave me the news of all the world. For two months I had been without letters, had seen no newspapers, had met no person with information from the outside. These are some of the things which they told me had occurred while I traveled across West Africa, indifferent to Europe and America: President Wilson had died; Lenin had died, and the city of Peter the Great had been renamed "Leningrad"; the Conservative ministry in England had resigned and a Labor government was in office under Mr. Ramsay MacDonald; England had accorded independence to Egypt; Ghandi had been released from prison in India; the monetary currencies of Europe were continuing their melancholy decline, and in some cases had ended in debâcle; plans for the Olympiad progressed hopefully; a French football team had defeated some other team; and a famous California sprinter had injured his leg and could not run in the international games!

Their long recital of public affairs made me acutely and unhappily conscious that my holiday already lay behind me; that I was soon to find myself absorbed again in the concerns of men of my own race; that I had about reached the turn of the road. Our "apéritif" was finished. Food was brought on. Quiet evening sounds came to us from the huts and camps that surrounded us. The soft hoof-beats of a drove of cattle could be heard passing along the road, guided southward to market by their Fula herdsmen. Immediately in front of me lay the belt of thick tropical forest, and beyond that the sea.

I treasure the memories of that evening with those

two kindly fellows as almost the last that I was to spend outside the confines of civilization. The next day brought me to the rail-head at Bouaké. Thence it was only a day's ride to the lagoons at Abidjan and to the coast at Grand Bassam.

CHAPTER XI

THE BLACK VETERAN

THE conquests which European leaders have effected over the African peoples, particularly since 1884, have been accomplished almost entirely through the use of Africans themselves. African soldiers have borne the brunt of the fighting, not only in French West Africa, but throughout most of the continent as well. In the British re-occupation of the Sudan under Kitchener, battalions of British soldiers were lent by the English Government to stiffen the lines of Egyptians and Sudanese, but, with this exception, South Africa, alone, has been a theater of warfare in which white troops were mainly employed. In the British-Boer war both sides disdained, or felt it to be impolitic, to employ colored forces, and the struggle became what Kipling's Indian character described as a "sahib's war". In German Southwest Africa, also, the German Empire used German troops to destroy the Herreros. Elsewhere, in the main, blacks have been enlisted to conquer blacks.

When Anglo-French relations were strained and competition over the frontiers of Nigeria and Dahomey became so acute as to threaten hostilities, both French and British organized Negro forces to settle this dispute. In British territory this was the origin of the famous "Waffs" (West African Frontier Force). The forces with which the redoubtable German leader, von Lettow-Vorbeck, for more than four years baffled the efforts of the Allies to gain possession of Tanganyika, consisted of 2,000 Germans and 14,000 Negro troops. They did not surrender until the Armistice, when nine-tenths of the German personnel had either perished or been taken prisoner.

The physical and moral qualities of the African assign him this rôle of lending himself to the European conquest of his own continent and his own race. He is naturally heedless of self, careless of the future, and readily impelled to adventure,—qualities that lie at the very bottom of a good soldier. He loves to place himself in obedience to a master whose superior qualities or position fascinate him. His vanity is moved by association with a white military leader, and instantly he despises his fellow countrymen serving under an African chief. He is capable of courage, great endurance and, in spite of a certain irresponsibility, of devoted attachment and fixed loyalty. Finally, his vanity, robust physique, exuberance, and incomparable power of enduring hardship, fill out the inventory of qualities that make him serviceable as a soldier.

From the beginning of the history of Africa, blacks have been recruited in the armies of other races. They appear to have figured extensively in the wars of Egypt, and have always been an element in the military power of Northern Africa. Thousands of black soldiers, at different periods, were recruited by the Berbers to make the arduous crossing of the Sahara and sacrifice their lives, in the conflicts of Ommiad or Saadian dynasties. The present sultan of Morocco is permitted by French authority to maintain a puppet army at Marrakech, composed of magnificent great blacks whose daily guard mount is one of the spectacles of that city.

Modern use of black soldiers is a matter of common knowledge, and has produced an impression leading to a great deal of exaggeration. The idea of reinforcing the man-power of France in European warfare by drawing on the millions of potential soldiers in the African possessions seems to be particularly due to the calculations and recommendations of General Mangin. By great exertions and the co-operation of the Wolof leaders of Senegal, the French Republic brought under the colors during the World War, 163,000 black troops of West Africa. Of these, 30,000 fought in the Somme. Their more effective use, however, was in Morocco, where, brigaded with Algerian and Moroccan troops, and stiffened by an element of the Foreign Legion, they constitute the forces, which have effected the subjugation of the Berbers of the Atlas.

France, in the creation of her colonial empire, is consciously following Roman leadership, introducing the Roman conception of common citizenship and common responsibility for the support of the empire. She has set out, I believe, to attract the native into the civilization which she represents, to make him feel his place in that civilization, and to be proud of his part, preferring it to any other status. In these steps, she is apparently succeeding beyond any other colonial power, and may, in the end, make the native as devoted to the defense of French culture and French empire as the ancient Briton or Spaniard was to the Roman.

From all I can judge, I believe that French policy is definitely determined upon using black soldiers wherever it is practicable to employ them, and to the utmost limits that economy of forces recommends. Nevertheless, this matter has been grossly exaggerated in countries outside of France, and its possibilities are much less than is ordinarily supposed in the United States. The raising of 163,000 black troops by the end of the World War, must be regarded as the maximum achievement that is practical under present conditions. After the war, an interministerial commission, presided over by Mangin, estimated that French West Africa could furnish 80,000 colored soldiers, 20,000 in each of three classes, under a three years' term of service, besides 20,000 voluntarily enlisted. So large a number was opposed by Governor-General Merlin, as occasioning undue economic sacrifices to a country wherein labor is insufficient. I judge that it is not considered practicable to keep more than 45,000 or 50,000 black soldiers serving with the colors during peace. Of these, a third constitute an army of defense for West Africa, and the balance are available for service in North Africa or elsewhere.

Preparedness for a larger use of black troops must rest upon the organization of reserves, and it appears doubtful to me whether a considerable reserve of native troops can be maintained among the blacks. The military education, and the effectiveness which it produces, rapidly desert a soldier when he leaves his organization and returns to his native village. All the way across the French Sudan I met discharged veterans of the French Army. In one fair-sized town the chief of the village reported that there were twenty-five ex-soldiers. These men, on hearing through the reports spread around by my cook and party that there was a white officer in camp, usually made haste to report themselves. Sometimes they would borrow a shirt and pin thereon a campaign medal or hunt up a steel helmet which they had brought back as a souvenir of military life. In some respects, their bearing and demeanor showed the training they had received. Some of them retained a little French caught with the easy linguistic apprehension of the Negro in the period of their service in the French Army. They could always tell me the number of their battalion or regiment, and those that had served in Morocco retained sufficiently distinct memories of that service. They had been quartered at Meknes or Taza. They had fought at Azrou or Kasbah Tadla. But the much smaller number who had seen service in France had only the vaguest impression of the experiences they had sustained. The memory of it was like a thick fog, full of din, turmoil and destruction, out of which they could not recall the name of a single French billet or a single battle sector.

Furthermore, as happens with ex-soldiers, these men were physically older than their age. Campaigning had prematurely advanced their years. They were invariably poor as Job's turkey, and had not been able

TRAVEL THROUGH THE "BUSH", FRENCH SUDAN

WITH FULA CHIEFTAINS AT BANGO, HAUTE VOLTA

STONE AND MUD DWELLINGS AT THE VILLAGE OF FIKO

It is built on an inaccessible mesa near Bandiagara by the Habés
seeking security against their more powerful enemies

HABÉS AT THE "MESA VILLAGE" OF FIKO

to translate the lessons of military life to their economic advantage in their native towns. I gained the impression that it would be of extremely doubtful advantage in ten years, or five years, after discharge from the colors, to summon these men again to the ranks. It would be better to start entirely with younger, fresher, and untrained men. It certainly takes a longer time to make an effective soldier of a Black than it does of a white man, and in warfare time is everything. The problem of equipment, of transportation, of supplying officers fitted by experience to command these forces, is a very difficult problem, and while I repeat that we may expect hereafter to see black troops in the French armies, wherever they can be advantageously used, it seems improbable that their numbers will ever rise to any considerable proportion of a European command.

There has been much British and American assertion, also, as to the effect produced upon black soldiers by their experience in European warfare, and their behavior after return to their own homes. Rumors have been spread that difficulties had occurred, and even that large forces were being retained abroad by France because it was feared to disband them in Africa. I saw no evidence of anything of this kind anywhere. One official, the administrateur of a *cercle*, did complain to me that the ex-soldier sometimes was a little difficult; but on the other hand a high official, responsible for the order of a great region, was positive that no increased difficulties whatever had been occasioned by the disbandment of the *tirailleurs* returned from Europe and Morocco.

The French have decreed the principle of liability of military service for all men of certain ages, and apparently they are applying the principle of a selective draft. In the southern part of Haute Volta, for instance, in the Cercle of Boromo, I saw no less than 500 young recruits being examined by a military board. They were young, athletic fellows and seemed to take their inspection with great good nature and hilarity. They evinced no unwillingness to serve and, so far as I could judge, were flattered and gratified by being passed into the service.

In the British colonies of the Gold Coast, and Nigeria, I found the opinion current that the extension of military liability in the French colonies was disturbing the native population, and causing emigration across the border into British territory. This may be true as regards certain migratory tribes, like the Fula, but on the other hand I think one should not trust too definitely the statements made by the black, when entering the colony of a different nation, as to the reasons for his move. In the first place, his change of residence may be purely temporary, a response to that restless instinct which is very strong in certain peoples of the Sudan. He may have come for trade or other expectant profit, and he is very quick to discover that one way to recommend himself with the officials of one nation is to complain of the system which he has experienced under the other.

My final impression is that the difficulty of creating in Africa a formidable army lies, not in the unwillingness of the black to leave home and become a soldier, but, as stated above, in economic and military limitations. As to the qualities of the black soldier when trained and properly led, all French officers, and, what is perhaps more significant, French *sous-officiers,* or non-commissioned officers, agree in awarding high praise. They say the blacks are brave, ready to follow anywhere, easily handled, peaceable among themselves, honest in their respect of one another's property, easily kept from pillage or misbehavior, and when given intelligible and thoroughly understood orders, responsible in executing them, providing no passage of time is permitted to take place. They are very resourceful in the fields, can throw up extemporized shelters where tents or billets cannot be provided, make the best of whatever food is at hand, and are supported against hardship by that irrepressible buoyancy and merriment which is one of the greatest assets of native character.

The military establishment that France maintains in West Africa, considering the newness of the conquest and the vast extent of territory, is moderate. It consists of two brigades of four regiments of black riflemen, one battalion of Colonial Infantry (European), the 6th Regiment of Colonial Artillery (European), one squadron of native *spahis* and one brigade of gendarmerie, colored. These forces form the defenses of Senegal, Guinea, Ivory Coast, Dahomey, Togoland, the French Sudan, the Volta, the Military Region of Timbuktu, Mauritania, and the Military Territory of the Niger. This corps of occupation in 1922 comprised 468 officers, 2,419 European troops and 13,363 native troops, besides a "replacement" force of 38 officers, 173 European soldiers and 1,868 native soldiers. The air service of West French Africa was organized by a decree of the French President in January, 1920. It is divided into two sections—one near Dakar and one at Bamako. Thirty-five landing fields are projected, of which twenty have been executed. The French Army appears to be leading all others in the employment of air craft in Africa.

CHAPTER XII

EXPLOITATION

THE creation of the present French colonial empire is the work of the Third Republic. In extent and importance, these possessions today rank second to those of Great Britain. The work of bringing so large a portion of the world under French authority was mainly accomplished in the years 1871-1914. These were, for France, years of chagrin and humiliation following defeat, of uncertainty with respect to the duration of the republic, and of international isolation. The achievement is all the more remarkable when viewed in relation to the period in which it was accomplished.

It is difficult to determine exactly the motives which spurred the French nation to so great an undertaking. To some it appears as an effort to redress the disequilibrium occasioned by defeat; an expression of the will to save France from sinking to the position of a second class power by building up overseas a new and greater France, to redress the increasing disparity between the strength of her population in Europe and that of competing nationalities. If this is a true explanation, it must be conceded, nevertheless, that the statesmanship behind the task was limited to a small number of French leaders. The French Chamber of Deputies was generally indifferent and supplied the means grudgingly.

It is the particular obsession of Socialists to ascribe the creation of colonial empire to the influence and insatiable greed of capitalistic organization. This explanation does not seem very plausible to one who travels far over the fields of newly won empires, and who sees business following rather timidly and reluctantly in the paths of adventurers who constantly press the frontiers of military and political control beyond the limits of trade. This is quite marked of French empire, wherein the charge constantly recurs that little economic advantage is developed from colonial conquest. It must at least be granted that the men who have done the work of penetration and exploration of unknown regions, the arduous task of conciliating some peoples and subduing others, of setting up French authority and French order, and making both recognized, have no connection whatever with capitalism and no share in its advantages. They are a mere handful of men who have sacrificed the charms and delights of their own country, to long years of hardship in sterile and lonely places, who have neither won, nor shown interest in gaining, great material rewards for their accomplishments, and who are stimulated by motives which the economic interpreter of history apparently fails to discover, but which are always present in French undertakings and which illuminate French history—love of adventure, of glory, of the power and honor of France. It is very difficult to foil such men or to restrain them. They progress in spite of the hesitations and timidities of their own government, of popular indifference and opposition, and in spite of extreme paucity of means. It is the fact that the French Republic, in spite of all the difficulties of the last half century, has produced such men, few in number but very great in soul, that explains why the French African empire of today embraces over forty-five per cent of the area of Africa and Madagascar.

The World War clearly has effected a change in the national attitude. During those exhausting years the French nation saw its combat and labor forces augmented by about a million men drawn from possessions overseas. It saw the harbors constantly filled with ships discharging upon the docks raw materials derived from the colonies. The nation, conscious of its numerical inferiority in Europe, has welcomed the doctrine that the French nation embraces not merely the forty million inhabitants of France but a hundred million souls within the entire national and imperial state. The ideal of building into one nation these diverse peoples of many parts of the earth may prove illusory, but few things in the world today are more interesting than the French effort to make it a reality.

However, the ultimate object of colonial acquisition in Africa is the expected advantage to the economic system of the sovereign country. Strategical and political motives may have determined the acquisition of certain possessions, but back of it all lies the realization, strongly felt now, that the continent of Europe is no longer self-sustaining, but must have great sources of raw materials beyond what Europe herself supplies, and markets outside of Europe, in which finished products can be advantageously exchanged. The highly complex social and industrial life of the present day has created this virtual dependence, so that any diminution of sources of supply or any interruption of the course of foreign trade produces immediate suffering. Europe and other portions of the temperate zone have become dependent upon certain products which the tropics alone supply. Food, clothing and manufactures, in our present civilization, require à constant provision of certain raw materials from the equatorial regions, and if they are not forthcoming, life in the temperate zones must be profoundly modified and its satisfactions curtailed.

Some tropical products have a very limited source, like the cloves and spices of the Moluccas, the hemp of the Philippine Islands, and India rubber, the source of which is practically controlled by the British Malayan possessions at the present time. Others are capable of wide diffusion and indefinite production. These conditions of modern economic life have stimulated the quest for regions, and particularly tropical regions, capable of a development that will make the country possessing them independent of other nations.

Possibly the only prominent country in the world that is not powerfully affected by such considerations as these is the United States, and American indifference to the possession of dependencies must be attributed to the fact that the country is nearly self-sufficing in what it produces. It is such a prodigious customer of

A BIT OF MURAL DECORATION IN THE HAUTE VOLTA COLONY

BUILDING MILLET GRANARIES, HAUTE VOLTA

BOBO WOMEN IN THE MARKET PLACE AT BANFORO, HAUTE VOLTA

all that can be manufactured that it does not feel the economic pressure toward politically controlled foreign markets that other nations feel. While dependent upon tropical productions no less than other countries, the United States has, to the south, a great tropical area whence it may conceivably derive all, or most, of its necessities of this kind, and within this region the American people feel there is little chance of their commerce being affected by the creation of "spheres of interest", or the erection of artificial barriers to their trade. The Monroe Doctrine assures to the national mind the maintenance of the "open-door" in tropical America. This situation may change in the immediate future, but it represents present conditions and probably explains American opposition to assuming further imperialistic responsibilities.

France is in a very different situation. While more nearly self-contained than most European nations, in the sense that she can more nearly raise her own food and support her civilization without dependence upon foreign products and manufactures, she needs not only foreign markets, but assured raw materials coming from outside, procurable for prices which she can pay. Upon the certainty of their delivery rests much of the prospect of her economic recovery and advance. It is under this sense of need that the French nation today expresses a more active interest in the economic possibilities of its vast empire.

Purely political considerations, glory and romance, the attraction for the French mind of bringing things into order and system, the resolution to keep the

French Republic in the forefront of powerful nations, have perhaps been the considerations most compelling in the spirits of the builders of her empire. But the more practical considerations of economic advantage may be expected to enter largely into the attention given to French possessions in the future. This tendency finds expression in the work of the recent Minister of Colonies, M. Albert Sarraut, *La Mise en Valeur des Colonies Françaises,* and this phrase, "la mise en valeur", meaning the realization of profit from all that France holds, is a phrase much encountered now in French conversation.

Considering only the colonies embraced in French West Africa, what economic profit does France realize and for what may she hope? African commerce began through trade or barter for things of native production or offering—gold, ivory, African pepper, palm oil, the palm kernel, and, for a long period, slaves. But the modern tendency is to survey the African field to see what products, not indigenous or usual to Africa, can be introduced, to stimulate production in these, and secure the advantage derivable from a large traffic in a few staple products, the production, transportation, and handling of which may be standardized. That this is possible in Africa is sufficiently well indicated by the development of the cacao industry in the British Colony of the Gold Coast. For some years, the Gold Coast supplied practically four-fifths of the chocolate consumed by Europe and America.

Out of the multitude of minor native-produced articles of trade which West Africa supplies for export, there are two articles which at the present time deserve special consideration. One is the peanut, which the English call the "ground nut", and the French, *arachide*. The loose soil of Senegal, though it is warm and dry during a part of the year, is nevertheless sufficiently watered by the seasonal rains, to be an admirable region for the production of the peanut. The labor involved in its planting and harvesting is very simple and not different from African methods of cultivation. Hence peanut-raising in Senegal has had a great boom. The building of the railway between Dakar and Saint Louis, and the extension of this railroad from the junction at Kayes eastward across Senegal to the upper waters of the Senegal River, has stimulated production over areas that, down to recent years, may have been quite unproductive and even uninhabited. The native Wolofs or Mandingos, and representatives of other peoples of Senegal, have been attracted by the price paid for this commodity into occupying these lands and raising the nuts. They are bought up directly by agents of the exporting companies and shipped out through the port of Dakar, and particularly through the port of Rufisque. On the train crossing Senegal I traveled a short distance in a compartment with two young Frenchmen who were going into the interior to buy peanuts from the native producers. They had with them two large flour sacks crammed with French currency notes of small denominations. They told me that the trade was very active, and the price demanded by the natives high— one franc a kilo.

The quantity of peanuts seems prodigious. The docks at both Dakar and Rufisque are covered with enormous piles of loose nuts sufficient at any time to fill the holds of a fleet of cargo boats. There seems to be an incessant movement of this product, from the interior to the ports, from the docks into the ships, and thence to Europe. The great demand for these nuts is not as an article of food in their roasted form, such as those which circulate in paper bags at baseball games in America, but for their yield of vegetable oil. This oil finds its way into salads and other dressings for which olive oil is supposedly used, and also into such industries as soap production and the numerous other purposes for which vegetable oil is in demand.

The second great staple which the French expect to derive from West Africa, and particularly from the valley of the Niger, is cotton. For a great while the United States has produced about three-quarters of the world's raw supply of this article. Nowhere in the world, apparently, can cotton be produced under such favorable circumstances of soil, acclimatized varieties, and available labor which understands the technique of its production, as in certain states of the American Union. Efforts carried out in many places and by many peoples to produce a rival to American cotton appear to be only moderately successful. Europe not only feels the disadvantage of being dependent upon a monopoly supply of this indispensable article, but believes that the American crop will become deficient for the world's needs. This seems to be partly due to our having nearly reached the limit of localities favorable for cotton cultivation, although new fields have recently been opened, as in Arizona and California, and also to the ravages of the boll weevil. The average American crop at the present time is about 12,000,000 bales, and the demand of the United States alone, if it was fully supplied, would seem prepared to consume ultimately this entire amount.

But the possible human demand for cotton goods may be greatly multiplied. The raising of the standard of life in such a country as India, whereby some hundreds of millions of helf-clothed people might aspire to decent garments, would alone represent an increased consumption of cotton which can scarcely be estimated. Cotton is the main article of clothing for the several hundred millions of China, where, dyed a fine Indigo blue, it is used as the common dress of the people in the warmer months, and properly quilted, forms the common garment for winter wear. The mills of Osaka, and the modern mills now erected at Shanghai create new manufacturing regions in Asia to compete with Europe for the increasingly inadequate supply of the raw article.

Under these circumstances, Europe has a great interest in the prospects of new fields for cotton production, and as England is the great cotton manufacturing country, English desire to hold Mesopotamia and to develop the Egyptian Sudan is understandable. If under British control these two great areas meet expectations, the world's extreme need may be greatly relieved. Unquestionably, not only the British Sudan, where, in Nubia and along the course of the Atbara, a new development of cotton raising is taking place, but also the Western Sudan would appear to have real promise as cotton producing localities. Throughout much of the Sudan, native cotton is raised by the blacks. It is grown in little patches hardly a hundred feet square. The article itself is inferior and of uneven staple. Even so, it is eagerly sought by traders in the Ivory and Gold Coasts and British Nigeria. It is spun and woven by the Sudanese into strong cloth and, at certain cities, as Kano, where the dyeing art seems to have reached the highest development, it is colored into beautiful, shimmering, glossy, dark blue and black fabrics, which have a wide and deserved renown.

The promise of this product as a great article of export lies in the introduction of a better variety than the indigenous plant, and in its cultivation on a large scale by European capital. The valley of the Niger, and especially that part susceptible of irrigation or of enrichment by the Niger's inundation, between Sansanding and Timbuktu, is an area capable of being transformed into a prodigious cotton field. The French have been giving attention to this prospect for some years. Six years ago they engaged the services of an American expert to acclimatize and introduce a suitable variety. This expert is a Dr. Forbes, a former student of the University of California. He had experience as a cotton expert in Egypt, and from that country entered the service of the French government in the Sudan. Supported by the preliminary studies of French irrigation engineers, Dr. Forbes has been carrying out experiments of great value. I encountered

him at Ségou, where the headquarters of this agricultural mission are located, and it was a rare pleasure
not only to meet a fellow American and a graduate
of my own university, to enjoy his hospitality and that
of his French companions, but to have the benefit of
his scientific observations upon the agricultural possibilities of the French Sudan. I would not desire
in anything I now say to anticipate the report which
Dr. Forbes himself will doubtless make upon the
result of this serious work which he has followed,
but some things which appear from his studies as he
communicated them to me, I think, he will not object
to having recited here.

In Dr. Forbes' opinion, the Sudan is capable of furnishing most, if not all, of the cotton required by
French mills. Extensive diversion of the water is
necessary, that the light and dry soils along the banks
of the Niger may become productive. Happily, the
flood of the Middle Niger coincides exactly with the
period of cotton culture, June to January. The Niger,
according to Sarraut, can furnish irrigation to an area
of from 400,000 to 450,000 hectares. In spite of the
fact that the inundation of the Niger is so extensive,
its overflow does not produce fertility at all comparable to that effected by the Nile in Egypt. The
waters of the Niger carry relatively little sediment.
Artificial enrichment of the soil will be necessary in
addition to irrigation. This may perhaps be furnished
by sowing with leguminous plants and consequent crop-
ping by cattle or swine. Labor is needed to develop the
cotton culture, to the extent of two laborers to a

hectare. The Sudanese population is the best of possible sources, but at present insufficient in numbers. It is thought that laborers from the great Mossi stock, or the Bobos to the south, may be attracted to the Niger valley by favorable conditions of employment.

Professor Gautier urges the building of the Trans-Saharan railway, not only to bring out the products of French West Africa, but to open the colonization of the Sudan to emigrants from Algeria, who, he thinks, are indispensable to its development. The Indian coolie might be brought in, but his presence would create problems, as has happened in Kenya and elsewhere, and it is extremely doubtful if the French government could be induced to favor immediate economic exploitation, at the price of future political and social difficulties.

At more than one point on the Niger, French efforts to plant and grow cotton have already begun. The most interesting of these is at Diré, only eighty-five kilometers south of Kabara. Here, a cotton growing establishment, the *Compagnie Cottonière de Nigerie* began operations some years ago. The country on the northern shore of this bend of the river is above the inundation, and extends northward in a great plain, the so-called "Sahel", that is covered with the thorny brush that fringes the sands of the Sahara. At Diré, for more than a half-mile along the Niger's bank, have been built very substantial adobe houses, each with an ample enclosure, as residences for the French employes, of whom there were about twelve, including a physician. At the end of this well-laid-out

street were yards containing tractors, great double
plows made in Breslau, lighter machinery, wagons, a
machine shop, and a very fine pumping plant which
raised from the Niger a magnificent stream of water.
This was being carried inland by a large canal, for a
distance of about seventeen kilometers, and along this
canal thousands of acres of land had been cleared and
leveled for the introduction of cotton. The crop of 1923
had brought, I was told, about 3,000,000 francs, and
was said to represent an excellent profit for these first
operations of the company.

The labor for this Diré settlement had been obtained
almost entirely from Timbuktu, whence several thousand people of the mixed inhabitants of that city have
been drawn by the attractive conditions of employment. They were living in extensive wards, composed
of grass huts, and each family group of huts was enclosed by a five-foot fence of poles and grass. The
blacks seem to greatly prize both the security and the
protection from intrusion that these little enclosures,
or zaribas, afford. Within the enclosure the family
activities group themselves, all quite orderly and cozy.

I wandered inland from this place for a kilometer or
more, and climbed a low sandy knoll, from which could
be seen the leveled and cleared ground of the company,
extending for some miles. Further to the north and west,
rose low hills. The knoll upon which I sat down to rest
proved to be a graveyard. The interments were rudely
marked by poles, or by the stretcher or mat in which
the body was brought to the ground. Amidst the debris
of this cemetery, which may have been an ancient as

well as a modern burial place, I found a heavy stone pestle, quite comparable to the long, well-shaped implements of the Pacific Coast Indians. Both the Sahara region and the Sudan at different places furnish remains of an African Stone Age, the explanation of which archæologists have not yet made.

The organization of industrial exploitation in tropical countries by strong companies, such as this cotton company of the Niger, has certain advantages over the venturesome attempts of individual men who undertake tropical agriculture. In the Philippines and elsewhere the experiment of developing plantations has been tried by isolated individuals, handicapped by trying conditions and by slender resources. Usually such attempts fail. To be successful, large resources are recommended. Men must be frequently relieved or replaced, and they must be held to a morale and a standard of life which it is difficult to preserve if a man is alone and dependent upon native society. The illness, death, or enforced removal of an individual engaged alone is the ruin of his enterprise. Co-operative and long-sustained effort seems to be the only sure way in which the white man can develop the agricultural possibilities of the tropics, and this, under our present capitalistic system, is furnished through the joint stock company.

There are some very impressive exhibits of the success of such corporate undertakings, as, for example, the United Fruit Company in the Caribbean. At any rate, it is only by the undertakings of corporations, especially organized for the purpose, that Americans will advance very far in the development of tropical plantations, for the type of American fitted to succeed in such work can only be attracted to it by the opportunities possible solely to large organizations, and in the American tropical countries, where political conditions are unstable, it is only a large and powerful corporation which can protect its rights against revolution, oppressive taxation, official interference, and possible confiscation. The policy of the American government, in recent years, has been such as to make precarious the situation of the small independent American planter. The indifference of the President and the Department of State to the fortunes of American investors in Mexico, after the revolution in that country took on an anti-foreign and confiscatory policy thirteen years ago, did not deprive the great American corporations in that country of considerable powers of self-protection, but it did ruin the thousands of American settlers whose means were limited and who were dependent upon themselves. These considerations would not obtain in the French Sudan, or in any French colony, where political authority is strong, and the great object is justice, but they were the reflections that came to my mind as I surveyed the beginnings of European activity in the valley of the Niger, and contrasted them with the broken efforts of Americans in tropical countries, where governments are frequently unstable and oppressive, and are not restrained from injustice by American public opinion or by the policy of our government.

The great bulk of Sudanese trade, as already stated,

is in articles raised by the native in his small, industrious fashion, and sold to middlemen, by whom they are exported. These middlemen in the Sudan are almost entirely of two classes: French trading companies, and Syrians. There are more than forty French houses organized for African trade, with establishments in Senegal, Guinea, the Ivory Coast, and, to a less degree, in the Haute Volta and Sudan. Most of these have their home establishments at Bordeaux, at Marseilles, or at Paris. These houses maintain branches at important trading centers, such as Bamako, Ségou, Mopti, Ouagadougou, or Bouaké. These trading posts seem to be well organized. The buildings cover spacious areas, with yards, warehouses, comfortable dwelling accommodations, and general stores. The shelves of these stores are filled with articles designed to attract the interest of the native, and to increase his economic desires. They include a variety of cotton goods, handkerchiefs, toilet articles, utensils, some preserved foods, and wines and liquors which I understand are sold only to whites. The supply varies in different localities, becoming more meager as one journeys toward the interior.

I spent some time in a trading establishment at Niafounké that particularly interested me. It was a branch of a well known French commercial company, the *Societé du Haute Ogooué*, a name derived from the Gaboon country, where this company first began its commercial enterprises. There was a single Frenchman in charge. The building entirely enclosed an interior *patio* which was shaded by trees, and had, in its center, a well. The outer walls were nearly everywhere blank and strong, and high enough to afford protection against a raiding force of pillagers. The enclosure was entered through a large gate, at one side of which was

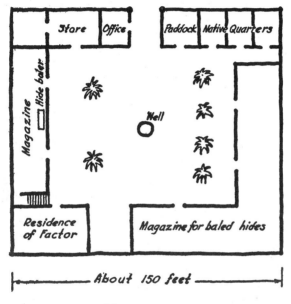

GROUND PLAN OF
TRADING POST AT NIAFOUNKE

a paddock for horses and, beyond it, native quarters. On the other side were an office, a general store, and a small liquor shop. On the sides of the enclosure were magazines, scales, and simple machines for baling hides, and at one corner a double-storied house which was the residence of the manager. The main article purchased here by this company is hides, and thousands of skins of cattle, sheep and goats, were crammed into the warehouses or had been formed by the presses into large bales, holding from 130 to 145 pieces, well sewed up in native sleeping mats, ready for shipment. The construction of this establishment reminded me vividly of old Fort Sutter at Sacramento, built eighty odd years ago in the Sacramento Valley, and then an outpost of the Spanish community strung along the coastal plains of California. The general plan of these two buildings, their defensive walls, their interior accommodations, were almost identical—as indeed they might be expected to be, since both were built after an architectural design inherited from a past in which the life of Europe and Africa commingled.

The Syrian merchants in the Sudan are organized in a much less impressive way. Sometimes they are mere itinerant traders, but in a few places they have fixed establishments, and show evidences of prosperity. When these people began to enter West Africa for purposes of trade, I do not know, but the close contacts of Syria with Marseilles, and their presence in that latter city contributed, doubtless, to introduce them into the French colonies. They are encountered frequently, traveling with natives and sharing native accommodations, living most frugally, and apparently content with smaller profits and a lower grade of enterprise than would satisfy the European. I found numbers of these Syrian traders also at Kano in British Nigeria, where they are very active in the great market which handles the peanuts brought in by innumerable little caravans. The French seem to be rather disturbed by the number and activity of these Syrian competitors, and doubtful as to what results their competition may bring. But I found the British attitude at Kano more favorable to them, as forming a necessary intermediate link in the chain of business.

Outside of these French companies and the Syrian traders, I found no white people in commerce over a very large area of the interior, for the representatives of the British, Italian, Belgian, and other nations in the French colonies are generally confined to the coast ports. I should, however, mention one more important factor in the trading operations of the Sudan. These are the itinerant Sudanese merchants, called *djoulas*. The word is not a tribal designation, but means "trader." They seem to be mainly Wolof and Mandingo natives, or at least they have had experience of life in Senegambia. They are invariably Mohammedans, and carry the influence of that faith wherever they trade. They are fine looking, well clothed men, and travel with horses, little troops of asses and a few servants, and sometimes they are accompanied by women and children. In the native markets everywhere one finds these men, their simple wares spread on skins in the shade of booth or tree. In addition to cloth, salt, and articles of ornament, they handle the kola nut trade, which is a very large part of the interior commerce of this part of Africa. The language spoken by these people is a sort of "trade tongue" and is likewise called "Djoula." It seems to be generally employed until one reaches the area over which the Hausa language forms the common medium of intercourse.

While trade and barter are obviously very much enjoyed by the Sudanese, and everybody is always carrying around something in the hope of sale or exchange, there is very little haggling. The Blacks seem to be, on the whole, a one-price people. If terms are not arranged between merchant and customer by a few gentle words of negotiation, the bargaining ceases and the purchaser moves on in the hopes of a better prospect. In all my own purchasing from natives, I found little or no disposition to reduce a first price, nor any disposition at all to question the adequacy of the very moderate sums paid for services or articles whose value is fixed by custom or local ordinance. The absence of annoyance through the importunity of the native is one of many attractive sides of Sudanese travel, and is appreciated by anyone who has endured the pestiferous importunities of the populations of the Mediterranean.

American trade with West Africa is limited, though it would seem to have opportunities. Here, as elsewhere, the most widely imported American articles are petroleum and gasoline, and, allied with the use of petroleum, I found natives in the upper Gold Coast bearing away from trading posts American lanterns, and showing every evidence of satisfaction with the serviceable article which has been devised to accompany our export of illuminating oil.

Mention has been made of the American consumption of the chocolate produced in the Gold Coast, and it may be added that a very great part of the mahogany now being taken from the exuberant forests of the

A "CAMPEMENT" OR REST STATION FOR TRAVELLERS

A group of natives called out for the corvee

A GRAVEYARD OF THE MOSSIS AT LAY, HAUTE VOLTA

French Ivory Coast is exported to America. The value of these great squared logs, as they lie on the beaches at Grand Bassam or elsewhere, is surprising. A single log of what is called "figured" mahogany, weighing about four tons, has been sold for as much as 80,000 francs. A single log has brought as high as £1,500, English money. Only about one per cent of mahogany logs, however, yield this exceptionally beautiful type of wood.

In the Ivory Coast I met a very interesting young Frenchman engaged in lumber exploitation on a considerable scale. He was, of course, a veteran of the World War, and had just received his cross of the Legion of Honor. He impressed me as being an exceptionally vigorous and intelligent man, from whom, in other countries, one would expect to hear criticisms of the administrative policy's attitude toward private enterprise. But instead of criticizing the slowness of the French economic development, his judgment was this: "These colonies will be all right if they are not developed too fast." This remark, coming from a private business man, seemed to me to support rather strikingly the French system of organizing strongly and surely the functions of government in advance of economic exploitation.

As a corollary to this cautious economic policy, the French exhibit an intention to keep the industrial development, so far as possible, in French hands. Unquestionably, their colonial enterprises could be stimulated if they were ready to invite the engineering and business experience and the capital of other nations. But this they seem not eager to do, preferring to keep enterprises to themselves, thus securing a smaller but an undivided profit. French business policy in this respect seems very different from that of the Belgians, with whom American brains and money are commencing to coöperate actively in the exploitation of the Congo.

CHAPTER XIII

GOVERNMENT

THERE are two broadly distinct policies employed by foreign nations in establishing their power in Africa: direct rule, and indirect. The latter policy consists in recognizing and using the authority of native rulers. It is utilized with striking results in Northern Nigeria, where it was developed by General Sir Frederick Lugard. That part of the Sudan had been prepared by native dominion for the introduction of British authority. The Fula people, two centuries before, had effected a conquest over the Hausa peoples of Northern Nigeria and on the thrones of such principalities as Kano, Katsura, and Sokoto, they placed chieftains of their own nation, called *emirs*, whose authority, once established, was long successfully exercised.

The Fula chieftains seem to have had considerable political talent. While exacting rulers, they showed themselves wise and humane. They had an instinct for organization, and an interest in the development of well-being. Nevertheless, by the time British influence began to penetrate Northern Nigeria, the days of strong and beneficent Fula rule were past. The power of the emirates had decayed. The iniquities to which African government is particularly subject had appeared, and the population was ready to turn from its allegiance to the Fula emirs to another set of masters who offered fairer prospects for the ordering of their lives.

Thus it was that with very modest military forces, and by the exercise of diplomacy, moderation, and firmness, General Lugard was able, in a short space of time, to supplant the native emirs who were hostile or resistant to British authority, or who were incapable of the able direction of public affairs. In their place were installed other chiefs who had a recognized right to the succession, and who accepted their emirates on the express condition of recognizing the British Crown as overlord, and of conducting the affairs of their states in accordance with the recommendations or requirements of British officers. The Fula emirs had established their theoretical title to the land, and this proprietorship passed by the very act of conquest from them to the British Crown and gave a legal basis for the present system of land taxation.

This, then, is the policy whereby, with singular economy of men and of expense, the British have been able to transform Northern Nigeria into the magnificent possession which it is today. The self-interest of the emirs is identified with British authority. The emirs themselves are zealous to suppress seditious movements among that part of the population susceptible to anti-foreign Mohammedan agitation, and the British administrators, through long training in the traditions of British empire, are masters of self-control, restraint, tact, judgment, and firmness.

Under this system it is to British interest to maintain the prestige and, up to a certain point, the authority of the emir, to satisfy the native population that their princes are respected and treated with consideration, and pains are not spared to support the dignity of these emirs, as long as their attitude is one of coöperation and obedience to British authority. Under such a system the machinery of native rule is, as far as possible, undisturbed. Justice and police are executed through native officials and in accordance with the native custom, which in Nigeria has been codified into law under the influence of Mohammedan jurisprudence. "Direct administration" is confined to technical services like railroads, communications, sanitation, and education, which are foreign to native experience and outside his theory of government. Such, in outline, is the system of indirect rule.

British Nigeria is considered to be the finest and most important crown colony of the British empire, and its capital, the city of Lagos, seemed the most pleasantly situated town which I saw on the coast of Africa. The harbor lies in the mouth of a river. Ships can enter over the bar and anchor close to serviceable docks along the shore. Government House, the residence of the governor, is a fine impressive building set amidst fresh gardens on the banks of the river. In this spacious and adequate palace, I was the guest of Sir Hugh and Lady Clifford. Sir Hugh was just completing an extended African experience, having previously been governor of the Gold Coast, and shortly afterward he was appointed governor of the island of Ceylon. But the greater part of his life has been passed in British Malaysia, and it is as a writer and scholar, in the field of Malayan life and language that he is best known. His career illustrates the pains taken by the British colonial service to select men of ability, train them while young, and then take full advantage of their experience as long as is possible.

Sir Hugh has an exceptional physique, unimpaired by exposures to the tropical jungle. It was his custom to arise before daylight and start work alone in his office. Here he would be found at his desk, a couple of hours later, with his tea tray before him, and much work already disposed of, while the morning was still fresh and young. On one occasion two hours before daylight he invited me to go with him to the slaughter-houses of Lagos, where he wished to satisfy himself that sanitary and humane regulations were being observed. He had taken great pains to improve the living accommodations of the government personnel in Lagos, and to establish splendid machine shops for the service of the port and the railroad. He had also convinced the Colonial Office of the desirability of forming a colonial legislative council in which the blacks are represented, and had just met this council for the first time.

In a British colony everyone sees that the person of a governor is treated with proper deference. He is the immediate representative of the King. There are certain small formalities that are not omitted. Yet this does not appear to indicate arrogance, but the reverse. Certainly no men in high official responsibility could be more approachable to all classes of people than those I met in West Africa governing colonies of the British empire. At Accra, the capital of the Gold Coast, the residence of the governor is in a famous old fortress, built by the Danes, and named Christiansborg. As the governor of the Gold Coast, Brigadier-General Sir Gordon Guggisberg, passed out of this fort, the bugle sounded, the guard fell in, and the full respects accorded the highest authority of the colony were rendered. This done, we got into an automobile, which the governor drove himself, and went off to chat in the market place with people of the town. The British believe in the value of symbols, and they do not neglect them. Neither do the French, for that matter, although their observance is of an entirely different character. An old Philippine colleague of mine, after visiting British India, returned to Manila with the statement that the "British governed that country with a white shirt-front." On being asked to state how the Americans governed the Philippines, he replied that "they did it with a baseball bat and a can of Hope-Deferred smoking mixture." The reader can put a lot of thought into these observations if he so desires.

The tropical coast comprised in British Nigeria probably had as wicked a history as any part of the African shore, before the' British took responsibility for it, and gave it a just and humane government. There are those who advocate a "hands off" policy with respect to all native territory, but they do not seem to know that their idea was tried for centuries with results unspeakably disastrous to the natives them-

selves, who were first enslaved, then robbed and de-
bauched with liquor under a *laissez-faire* system by
which no European power accepted the burden of government. If the "hands off" advocate insists that this
was due to the white man's rapacity and cruelty, can
he say how he will check that rapacity and cruelty
except by establishing authority on the spot? The slave
trade can be banned from the seas but can *all* trade
be barred between our own race and races incapable
of ordering their affairs in competition with our own?
No one who knows the history of Lagos and of Old
Calabar wants to see British rule removed.

Instructive as this British capital of Lagos is, the
frightful torrid humidity made me happy to escape
northward up the railroad to Kano. This railroad is
an impressive piece of British achievement, connecting
Northern Nigeria with the sea, but its service did not
appear to be as comfortable and serviceable as the
costs of transportation on it would justify. It is used
not only for reaching Northern Nigeria, but by French
officers enroute to Zinder, the capital of the Military
Territory of the Niger which lies just beyond, and
there were several French officers making the trip in
the car by which I journeyed.

I was fortunate in my compartment-companion—a
young Scotch physician, a graduate of the University
of Aberdeen, full of loyalty to his old institution and
the memory of its illustrious· men. He had just entered
the colonial service, and after a few weeks of preliminary experience at Lagos, was under orders for Kano.
He insisted on my being his guest at Kano, and I had

interest and pleasure in watching him establish himself. He belongs to a race that has covered the whole globe with its adventures, whose men can take care of themselves in any clime and under any circumstances. All this is in their blood, and it showed itself in my friend's entire familiarity with his problem. He had an immense quantity of supplies—boxes and boxes of those beautifully tinned provisions which it is the business of British grocers to sell to colonists, and which he had brought with him from home. He had a motor bicycle. He had three servants whom he had engaged at Lagos, uniformed and trained. He had laboratory equipment with him, and, within a day of our arrival, had installed it in one room of his adobe bungalow. It was only a matter of hours after our arrival before his home was arranged, the little native hospital taken over, and he was sewing up wounds and administering medicines to patients who awaited him.

Northern Nigeria is the most populous and the most advanced area of the Sudan. Twenty million people inhabit this northern plain, and Kano is the largest and most thriving native city that I saw. Its ancient mud walls are some twelve miles in circumference. They enclose an area not only adequate for the crowded wards of the city, but with space for the refuge of the flocks as well. A dozen gates open in all directions through these walls. In and out of them at all hours of the day pass troops of natives—Tuareg camel-men from the desert, parties of Kanuri people with long horned cattle from Lake Chad, innumerable natives with droves of asses and parties of galloping Hausa and Fula horsemen. A great traffic in native cotton, in peanuts, and in other products centers at Kano. Within the walls are the palace of the Emir, mosques, schools, thronged markets, and community after community of manufacturers producing the famous leather work and dyed cotton goods of Kano. The area around the city, inhabited by more than a million and a half of people, constitutes one of the several "residences" of this northern area, all of them governed, as previously stated, under native princes with British supervision and control.

The French, in developing their colonial empire, have not generally employed indirect rule. In Morocco and in Tunisia, which have the status of protectorates, and in which the French Republic is practically in the position of a trustee for native vested rights, and for foreign interests as well as for French, indirect rule through the sultan or bey has been followed. But one gains the impression that it is less an actual fact than is native rule under British forms of protectorate.

In French West Africa, on the contrary, the French have adopted a system of government based upon the direct authority of governor and district officers. In defense of their direct administration, it may be observed that the native political conditions in Senegal or the Niger valley offered no such favorable opportunity for the perpetuation of native kingships as in Nigeria. Most of the Sudanese kings, the *alemáni,* were not only tyrants incapable of good government, irresponsible to even native ideas of justice, but they resisted French penetration by protracted warfare which completely exhausted their resources. The conquest effected their effacement.

As fast as the French made themselves military masters of this territory, they introduced their own administration, which follows precisely the lines of the strong centralized government of France that was given effective and permanent form by the genius of Napoleon. The several colonies,—Senegal, Sudan, Haute Volta, etc., are each presided over by a lieutenant-governor, who is the center of administration. He has a small but competent staff, including a *chef-de-cabinet,* who closely parallels a chief of staff in military administration. The chief of cabinet is usually a young man, intelligent, active, and permeated with a sense of discipline and order. A large part of the details of government of the colony passes over his desk. The secretarial work of the colony is under his hand. The governor, however, is himself in close contact with every branch of the administration and every problem of government, and on all matters of importance he himself makes the decision. Associated with the colonial governor in all colonies except Senegal, there is a "council of administration," whose advice on certain matters must, by law, be heard, though not necessarily followed. These councils of administration, according to recent decrees of the French Government, comprise the colonial governor, as president, the general secretary, a legal officer of rank—either a magistrate or a "procureur" of the Republic, the ranking military officer of the colony, the chief of one branch of the service designated each year by the governor, the president of the chamber of commerce of the colony, if one exists, and four "notables," two of them French citizens and two, "French subjects," that is, native chiefs. In each colony, also, there is an administrative tribunal called the *Conseil de Contentieux Administratif,* of which the governor of the colony is president and which, in accordance with French administrative law, decides cases of jurisdiction and complaints against official action.

There are certain heads of services, who at all times have direct access to the governor, and while the system of a chief of cabinet spares the chief executive a large amount of detailed administration and leaves him free for consultation or deliberation upon important matters, his time is nevertheless very fully occupied— so fully occupied, indeed, that I gained the impression that an insufficient time is left for leisurely travel and inspection of his jurisdiction. I thought I could detect a feeling of concern at the idea of being many hours absent from headquarters, unable instantly to make response to the summary demands for report and action that come over the wire from the office of the Governor General at Dakar. The governors or lieutenant-governors of colonies are civilians and belong to a professional class. They have reached their positions by training and an experience which embraces not only the continent of Africa, but the great possession of Madagascar and the empire of Indo-China.

The territory of a colony is divided into large areas of administration, called *cercles.* At the head of each one is an official, almost always a civilian, called the *administrateur*. He may have an assistant administrateur, a younger man in training for higher responsibilities, but in some cases he works alone, unaided by European collaborators and dependent only upon trained native help, which includes several educated black clerks and interpreters, and orderlies, called *brigadiers*, who are discharged non-commissioned officers of the native army. These are tall, splendid black men, who wear the uniform of the *Tirailleurs*, are instant in their obedience to the orders given and are altogether one of the finest class of native men of this grade that I have ever seen. There is also at the "chief place" of a *cercle* a detachment of native gendarmes, a native telegrapher or two, a native postmaster, and other trained blacks in charge of storehouses, the jail, labor parties and markets. The post of the administrateur is at a central town, which gains in importance by reason of being the local capital. Invariably the quarters of this post lie outside the native community and have been constructed in a favorable location upon a rather elaborate and dignified plan. The houses are of mud, but are spacious, well built, usually of one story. They are protected by deep arcades which shut out the African sun. Even where there is a single administrateur, there is a group of public buildings, one for a residence, another for the offices, a third for the court of justice, another for the local school.

The French carry to Africa, and to these little posts, their passion for tree planting and gardening. The streets and squares and surroundings of these quarters are invariably planted to trees and shrubbery, and wherever a few years of time have permitted their growth, a luxuriant and beautiful result has been attained. In fact, the setting of some of these posts is a veritable bower—an oasis in the midst of the monotonous brush and sand. Not all the planting is ornamental. Every French post has an admirably cultivated garden. More than once I was favored with baskets of the choicest vegetables. The Frenchman carries his garden with him into Africa, and sees to it that his table does not lack the indispensable *salade*. In the Haute Volta I found several places where wheat is successfully grown in little hand-cultivated plots, the grain milled and baked into crusty French bread, all the processes effected by native hands trained in these little posts.

Economy has compelled the French to make the areas of these *cercles* large, and the work of the administrateur is correspondingly heavy. The entire colony of Senegal, for example, has seventeen administrative *cercles*, the Sudan, twenty-one, the Haute Volta, nine. The *cercle* of Ségou has a population of 225,000 souls, Dedougou, 422,000, Mossi, 1,550,000. The work of the administrateur is laborious and confining. He rises early and after a cup of coffee repairs at once to his office. Here, within and outside of the administration building, there are assembled, every day, hundreds of natives waiting for his judgment. It was an interesting experience to sit beside these administrateurs through the hours of a long, hard-pressed forenoon and watch their work. Here was a party of blacks desiring to leave the *cercle* and go on a trading expedition into the interior or perhaps into British territory. Their request had to be heard, discussed, its limits inquired into and defined. A written permit, quickly prepared by a native clerk, was then signed and issued. Next came a party of village people who, heedlessly or wantonly, had destroyed the sparse forest which must be jealously guarded as a measure of protection against the progressive desiccation of the Sudan. The complaint is heard. The men are impressively chidden or reproved or perhaps even given jail punishment. Then there are native village chiefs to be instructed with respect to road work or public improvements or to the furnishing of the *corvée*, the labor of which amounts to eight or ten days a year, and is required of each head of a family. The business is interminable and usually pressing. Offenses, including crimes, have to be inquired into and native policemen sent out to make arrests. Taxes must be collected, the annual payment of which takes the form of a small poll tax. The business, I judge, constantly tends to expand. While it must be largely settled offhand, the requirements of French administration impose upon the administrateur the making of what seem to be over-elaborate records. The paper work is large and, I should think, cumbersome. *Déjeuner,* at noon, finds the administrateur already a weary man, but back to the office he goes in the afternoon to clear up the mass of business unsettled in the morning. Again, I gained the impression that here are men so overworked, so hampered by details, that travel, visits of inspection to important villages and towns, and leisurely perambulation through their jurisdictions is impossible. The highly centralized system of French government binds the local official, as it does the governor, to his desk and the telegraph instrument. The authority of these men, while great, is sharply defined by a code. Above them is the authority of the lieutenant-governor, whose orders may not be questioned, and who must be implicitly obeyed. The discipline of the service is strong.

The type of men engaged in this work varies. Here is a veteran of the war, with one limb lacking; there a former soldier of the French colonial army, who has advanced by successive grades to his position; there a young graduate of a French university, still exhibiting, in the midst of a rugged life, the refinement of the intellectual classes. All these men, whether, from an American standpoint, well educated or imperfectly educated, seemed to be animated by unflagging devotion to their work, by zeal for their tasks and by firm belief in its prospects. Ill health, moreover, was rare. Nearly every French official whom I met in the interior was sunburned, vigorous, and the embodiment of physical energy. The habits of these men are temperate. At *déjeuner* and dinner, and sometimes, in that charming twilight hour preceding the evening meal when the party, whatever it may be, gathers in the open air about a table for the *apératif*, a little wine or vermouth is taken; but invariably the liquor is mixed with a copious supply of water. I remember at one of the larger posts where there were several French families and where I was entertained at a delightful luncheon, the discussion had mainly to do with the

A BAND OF PERFORMERS AT THE FÊTE OF SEGOU

The objects at the right, each with two slender horns and shaggy mane, are masks

A VILLAGE CHIEF WITH HIS WELL-EQUIPPED HORSE

The chief carries a sabre, indicative of his official position

FRENCH BUILT PUBLIC MARKET AT MOPTI

In the construction of public buildings the government follows the native architecture of the Sudan, and improves upon it

THE "RESIDENCE" AT SEGOU

inexplicable performance of the American Nation in enacting prohibition, yet two of the four men and one of the three ladies were teetotalers.

Within the *cercle*, the territory is divided into districts, and these districts, into village communities. In each district is a native chief, who is held responsible for the peace and order of his region, and in each village there is a village chief. These chiefs are designated by the administrateur and their authority flows from him. Nevertheless, all the village chiefs with whom I discussed the matter told me that they were the sons and grandsons of men in similar position, that they considered their office permanent, and they expected to be succeeded by one of their own sons. These chiefs differed much in their appearance of well being. Some were, obviously, quite as poor as the poorest of their village compatriots. Others, and particularly in the Mossi country, were surrounded by little retinues and evidently possessed such means as a well-to-do man in the Sudan may have. They were all, however, as I have above testified, instant in the performance of such duties of attention to a foreigner traveling through the country as are laid upon a chief and his community, and the service seemed to be offered happily and ungrudgingly.

There is no doubt that French authority is strongly organized and ably exercised. There is no doubt, either, that it is discharged at a minimum of expense. I think it unlikely that under this system there can occur any considerable abuse of power or any distortion of justice or gross corruption on the part of a European official. The French standards in these respects are severe and high, and, above the formal requirements of their office there seemed to me to be, in the convictions of all these men, a fine sympathy for justice and an enthusiasm for "the liberty, equality, and fraternity" which the French Revolution has indelibly imprinted upon French character.

The manner of these officers in dealing with the natives is striking. Conversation is terse and rapid; orders are given in decisive military tones. The air of authority is strong. Nonetheless, the pride of the native is never wounded. If he is reproved, it is not done in a vulgar or bullying way. The self-respect of the native in his contacts with these officials seems to be not merely protected but stimulated, just as the self-respect of a soldier gains through contact with an exacting but just officer.

It was on the side of the administration of justice only, that I heard the French officials speak with some concern about the system. Considerable reliance for the judicial resolution of native difficulties necessarily must be placed upon the black. In each village, there is a native tribunal formed by the village chief. He plays the rôle of a conciliator in disputes that are brought to him, but his sentence is only valid if it is accepted by the parties interested. If, through the hearing of the village tribunal, an agreement is not made, the litigants can take their difficulty to the "tribunal of the subdivision." These native courts are created by an ordinance or *arrêté* of the governor and are composed of three natives—a president and two assessors

—chosen from a list of five "notables." These are real native courts of first instance. Where tribal customs vary, there is a special tribunal subdivision for each ethnic group having a different customary law. From these native courts there is an appeal to the "tribunal of the *cercle*," which is composed of the administrateur as president and two native assessors, chosen from a list of four notables. Where the tribunal of the *cercle* imposes a heavier penalty than five years imprisonment, the decision is reviewed by a special chamber of the Court of Appeal of French West Africa. The above description applies only to the administration of justice for the native. There is a separate judicial system for Europeans.

I recall one especially interesting afternoon spent with the natives of the village of Bango just over the boundary of the colony of Haute Volta. This was a Fula community and the chief, a man of great dignity, was described as the chief authority over all the Fulas in this region. He was a tall, commanding fellow of middle age, and carried a light sword with the arms of the French republic emblazoned on the hilt. He also wore a rosary which he used in counting up for me the number of men in that village who had served in the army. The men who attended him were likewise Fulas, and one of them showed me a number of papers to which he obviously attached importance. One was a gun license, *"permis de porte l'arme,"* given him by the administrateur of the *cercle,* in the name of the governor of the colony. Another document was a letter in Arabic character, addressed in French to *"Monsieur*

Sambo Salip, Président du Tribunal de Subdivision Ouahigouya." The amenities of the occasion included the exchange of gifts, the chief furnishing me with a fine, fat sheep; target shooting with my arms, with which these blacks showed some familiarity, and the discussion of many small topics of government and community life. These Fulas were a fine, impressive body of men, all Mohammedans, of course, and, so far as I could observe, they were content with the way in which their life was ordered, although French rule has meant restraint to these aggressive people, whose historic rôle has been that of invaders among aboriginal stocks which they formerly dominated.

It will be apparent from the above that the French respect and utilize native organization and native leadership, and that while progress in this direction may not be rapid, they are introducing a "régime of coöperation" into their government of West Africa. The policy of according the native a share in his own political affairs has gone farthest in the colony of Senegal, where the blacks are represented by such advanced stocks as the Wolofs. As the result of the contribution made by the people of Senegal to the War, some rather surprising bestowals of self-government have been made. Four communes have been given such autonomous powers as are generally accorded by French municipal law,—St. Louis, Goree, Dakar, and Rufisque, —and the native inhabitants of these communes and their descendants, were made French citizens by a law of the 24th of September, 1916. As the municipal councils are elected by the votes of all citizens, it results that the councillors are blacks. French citizenship may also be acquired by naturalization in French West Africa by natives who are literate in French, or who have accomplished a period of military service in a regular corps, or by any native who has been decorated with the cross of the Legion of Honor or with the Military Medal, or who has rendered signal service to France or to his colony.

Furthermore, Senegal possesses a "colonial council" reorganized by a decree of the 4th of December, 1920, consisting of forty members, of whom twenty are elected by French citizens dwelling in the colony, and twenty are native chiefs chosen by an assembly of the chiefs of electoral districts. This council meets once a year, chooses its own president, and has very much such powers as are exercised by "general councils" in the departments of France. Finally, Senegal is represented in the French Chamber of Deputies at Paris by a representative chosen by the majority vote of all French citizens and, therefore, a black. By such local arrangements as these it is clear that the French have not hesitated to accord to the native of ability and loyalty, rights and a position comparable to those of French citizens generally. During the course of the War, when other considerations were subordinated to the purpose of securing the largest possible voluntary enlistment of natives of French West Africa, the deputy from Senegal was sent "on mission" to Africa and given diplomatic rank and high ceremonial precedence. The incident did not pass without protest and some awkward consequences, but the dignity that had been accorded to this Senegalese was sustained by the government of the Republic.

What finally are the position and functions of the governor-general? By this office the French have effected a unification of several colonies which differ from one another in their history, the length of time in which they have been under French control, and other important respects. They have, at the same time, sought, by the development of this supreme colonial office, to solve an old dilemma of colonial government, namely: How to make the authority of the man on the ground commensurate with his heavy responsibilities, and at the same time assure his adherence to the policies and conduct of office prescribed by the home government. This latter responsibility, under most systems of colonial rule, is exercised by a ministry at the home capital. But the distance is too removed either for effective oversight or for sympathetic understanding of the difficulties involved in local administration. In creating a governor-general the French government has shifted this responsibility to him. He has no direct responsibility for territorial administration. This function is given to the lieutenant-governor of each colony. He is detached from the most vexatious and the harassing details of direct administration. He has, however, the full power of the French Republic to enforce the policy of his government over the subordinate governors of colonies. He alone has the right of correspondence with the Minister of Colonies at Paris, and with other ministers of the home government. He has control of the French military forces in West Africa, and the right to direct the use of the naval forces on station there. He has important powers of appointment, of discipline and of legislation. A few of the services which require to be unified for all French West Africa are directly under his administration. But, as stated above, he has no special responsibility for any of the colonies making up the whole. The plan seems to be a logical solution of an old political difficulty—but the French have reached their present treatment of the matter less by logical thinking than by a long process of trial.

The effectiveness of any system of government is dependent upon the excellence of its communications. The French have taken great pains in this field. There are nine distinct postal and telegraph districts, one for each of the nine colonies of the governor-generalcy; but unity of direction and a constant examination of the general interests of the service are assured by the governor-general. The service maintains 282 offices or bureaus, only thirty-two providing postal service alone. The telegraphic net in 1923 comprised 23,278 kilometers, or nearly 15,000 miles of wire and installations. There are French submarine cables uniting Dakar with the port of Brest and branches connecting Dakar with Conakry, Monrovia (Liberia), Grand Bassam and Cotenou. Another French cable connects French West Africa with Morocco. In addition to this wire communication, an important system of radio telegraphy has been installed. By these stations Dakar communicates not only with such important interior cities as Timbuktu, but with distant Saharan posts such as Zinder, N'Guigmi, Agades, north of British Nigeria, and with such Mauritanian stations as Atar, Chingueti, and Port Etienne. At Bamako there was under construction an intercolonial radio station designed to be of great power, and to effect direct and bilateral communications with France.

CHAPTER XIV

THE BLACK

IN these final paragraphs I set down some impressions of the types and qualities of the native men and women encountered on this trip through the Land of the blacks. The origin of the African stocks is enveloped in mystery. The base is furnished by the "true negro," who is recognized as one of the fundamental, distinct, and original types of the human species. The negro may or may not have been the oldest sub-species of our race, the original product of animal evolution to be endowed with human qualities, but there are facts which suggest this,—such as his extraordinary dispersal, from Melanesia and Papua, across the Indian Ocean, to the continent of Africa. If the human race arose in the tropics, and palaeontology offers some support to this thesis, there is additional reason to suppose that Primitive Man was "black," that is, highly pigmented, so that his cellular structure might be protected against the direct rays of tropical light. But in other than tropical regions, mankind developed different types which lack dense pigmentation in climates where the sun ceased to be pernicious and became a stimulant to physical and mental activity.

However these races,—white, yellow, brown, red, black—to give them the popular designations, that

have been current since the writings of Blumenbach—
came to be, in few parts of the world have they remained wholly separate and distinct. The fundamental
biological fact in regard to mankind is that the varieties successfully interbreed and produce new types that
multiply to great numbers as the result of the mingling.

There seems to be an instinctive movement of humanity toward the equator, away from the cold and
toward the sun. This carried white and brown types of
mankind, ages ago, into Black Africa, with the result
that the African race is true Negro only in a limited
region, namely, the Guinea Coast and the northern portion of the basin of the Congo. The broad belt of the
Sudan, as has been repeatedly stated, is inhabited by
peoples who are blends of Negro blood with various
elements coming from the north, and perhaps from the
valley of the Nile. It is of this mixed stock that I wish
to give certain impressions. It embraces many tribes,
languages, and cultures—Wolofs and Mandingos in
Senegal, with whom mingle "Moors", Berbers, and
Toucouleurs, Bambaras, Songrais, Habés, Mossis, and,
further east, in Northern Nigeria, Hausas and Kanuris.
Mingling with these are the nomadic Fulas. Transplant-
ings, usurpations of land, slave raiding, and, finally,
the great peace of the land established by French and
British authority, have created an extraordinary commingling of these and other original tribal groupings.
This commingling gives us the blacks of the Sudan.

I have elsewhere spoken of my impressions of the
physical endowment of this race—its robust physique,
fine stature, endurance, and fortitude. These qualities

are apparent in women as well as in men. The busy, chattering groups splashing on the shores of the Niger, washing their clothing in gourds and pots, tending their little plots of vegetation, contain some of the most robust types of women to be found in any race. Their appearance is rendered perhaps not more beautiful to our eyes, but more striking, by the eccentricity of their adornments, the singular and varied ways in which the hair is arranged,—braided into balls and coxcombs,—the ornaments of brass, of amber beads or of stone that hang about their necks and on their limbs. Yet among such groups of veritable Amazons, athletic, voluble, untouched by diffidence or the grace of feminine modesty, one sees more delicate types of women—slender, retiring, with sensitive expressions, delicate features, and airs of native good breeding that are really charming.

To other forms of adornment, the Sudanese add the widely current practice of scarification. These marks, on face or body, are tribal designations and doubtless arose out of the necessity of such instant forms of recognition, but they have taken serious, and perhaps indelible, hold on the native mind, and as one goes southward across the Sudan, they become constantly more common, more elaborate, and more dreadful. In one tribe, for instance, the face-scarification, in addition to a series of cuts radiating across the brow from the root of the nose, consists of an elaborate ladder, carved, on each cheek. In an active little market place, under widely spread thorn trees, I came one day upon two little boys perhaps three

years of age, upon whom this multilation had been
recently performed. Their faces, covered with frightful cuts and wounds, were really dreadful to behold.
They clung close to their mothers, subdued, pensive,
and pitiful. The thought of the shock to an infant
nature suffered by such an ordeal haunted me for
days. One could write a very elaborate book upon this
singular practice of scarification in the Sudan.

I have, under the topic of *The Black Veteran,* sufficiently emphasized the warlike propensities of the
Sudanese. This subject has been artistically handled
in Kipling's poem of the "Fuzzy-Wuzzy." I can do
little to emphasize it further, but undoubtedly it is a
fact to be considered repeatedly that here is a great
militant people, with an instinctive love for adventure
and for the foray, with a passion for the pomp and
panoply of war, and with a capacity for dutiful obedience equal to any armed men.

The bearing and demeanor of the blacks is more
serious than I had expected. They are not sportive nor
gay. They do not indulge in "horse play," nor do they
spontaneously burst into song. I do not mean that
these people are morose, as the Negroes appear to be
in some islands of the West Indies; but they do not
furnish those laughing, rollicking groups that one meets
on the levees of New Orleans, or wherever colored
people congregate in America. In fact, while this is
only an impression, I offer it here, that in spite of the
severities and limitations on the black man's life in the
United States, he is nowhere else so joyous, so ready
for mirth and for music, as he is in our own country.

The relative infrequency of singing and of music disappointed me. My bearers never chanted as they strode. They did not sing around the camp fires or on the boats.

At Ségou, the town was *en fête* for the visit of the Governor General. Early in the morning the river was full of canoes, in which native boys were swiftly paddling chieftains and retainers to the landing places. The streets of the town were filled with cavalcades of horsemen, with companies of musicians, with detachments of militia, armed with flint-lock rifles and ancient weapons,—the residue, doubtless, of those native armies which the French were long and deliberate in conquering, but which they have most effectively subdued. Dozens of village and district headmen had come in with their followers to pay their respects and enjoy the gala occasion, and the total number ran into many thousands. The musicians had fifes, odd little banjos, and above everything else, that great instrument of music and of rhythm, the drum. These entertainers were accompanied by troups of comely young girls. But the music and the dancing were more formal than exuberant.

Lying on my cot in the open air one night at Ouahigouya, I was awakened by the distant reverberation of· drums and the clamor of revelry. It went on hour after hour, and, in the course of the night, unable longer to resist its attraction, I forsook my bed and stumbled for a mile or more across the plain to a midnight scene of dancing and hilarity. Hundreds of people had gathered in the gloom around small and insufficient bonfires, to watch and to applaud the performers. Both men and women engaged in these dances—stooping, stamping their feet, swaying their bodies, circling in dance formations, to the boom of the drums and the higher notes of the wind and stringed instruments of the musicians. But such free and wild enjoyment as this was less frequent than I had expected to find.

The troubadour is rare. On the banks of the river at Mopti, I came one day upon the drollest little musician —a true Negro, snatched by some fate from the forest, hundreds of miles to the south. He was a grotesque little man, bent and solemn, streaks of gray mingling with the tight wool of his curly head. He had an odd little guitar with a couple of strings. On this he picked an accompaniment and sang a funny plaintive little air in the highest of falsetto keys. The stalwart, white-robed Sudanese who surrounded him were delighted with his performance, and were convulsed with hilarity. But he could be induced to furnish us with only a very limited amount of his quaint entertainment, and although one of the Sudanese gave him a half-franc, he presently ran away and could not be persuaded to return.

Why is it that this native Sudan population lacks generally the great consolation and support to the soul which song and music afford? Have these expressions, so invariably associated with the Negro, been suppressed by the centuries of anguish which make up the history of the Sudan? Has character become somber under the brutalizing horrors of war and slavery? Have the sword and the chain here suppressed the inherent buoyancy of the Negro? Or is this more sober character the result of mingling with the gloomy and pitiless white stocks drawn from the Sahara and the northern mountains of Africa?

The family group in this part of Africa or elsewhere is the unit of society, and the authority of the man over his polygamous household is enormous. So far it has been little relaxed by the introduction of the white man's justice. But it is male authority rather than male attachment. Family affections are built far less about the instincts of fatherhood than about the extraordinary fondness that exists between mother and child. The devotion of a black mother for her babe, the undiminishing loyalty and affection which men and women give to their mothers, seems to me the most touching thing in African society. It is not the mere animal attachment of the female for its young, for it does not wane after the period of nurture passes, but persists through maturity. It is perhaps the best ground of appeal to the higher nature of the black, and the soundest basis upon which his social relations may be improved. I do not mean to suggest that fathers are generally indifferent to their children, but the finer attachment of father for child and child for father does not appear, I fancy, in polygamous society. In the course of human development, it doubtless took a great while to bring the father to a recognition of his own child, and to a concern for his own child approximating that of the mother, and in Africa the uncertainties which surround male parenthood weaken the force of this interest.

Africa is a continent of debased religious practices. Perhaps no place in the world, not even in Malaysia, where ghosts haunt the lives of primitive men, are the terrors of the invisible more conjured upon or made the occasion for more frightful practices than among the Negro race. I have already mentioned the effect of Islam upon African peoples, and the progress of this religion in the Sudan. It seems to be the opinion of many writers that knowledge of this religion does not extend very far among the blacks, that their practice of it amounts to little more than an abjuration of pork and wine, the performance of a few prayers, and the profession of belief in One God and his Prophet Mohammed. This may be granted without diminishing our recognition of the powerful effect of this religion, as a liberator from pagan superstitions. The primitive apprehension of the tenets of Mohammedanism by the black is probably no more primitive than the grasp of Christian principles by masses of people in European countries. Undoubtedly, pagan practices and beliefs keep hold upon the population even after Mohammedanism has been professed. Islam and fetishism mingle throughout the Sudan and even in the Valley of the Niger. Landing one day from my boat on the Niger at a little village not far below Koulikoro, in the course of hunting, I came upon a "sacred grove," an institution widely revered in this country, and typical of fetish ceremonial. It was a thick mass of trees and jungle, with a circumference of perhaps a hundred yards. The ground around the periphery was cleared and carefully swept, like a well tended road.

Wandering around it, I came upon an opening through the shrubbery, which led to the very heart of the grove where there was a small clearing. There was nothing striking here except a great covered jar, placed in the middle of the enclosure. When I irreverently lifted the cover from this jar, I found it to be well lined with imprisoned lizards, myriapods and other vermin. I called a great strapping orderly, and took him with me into this grove; but the minute he saw the cleared space and the fateful jar, he fled. This sort of thing, he said, was "gris-gris," the polyglot word for African superstitions, and it would be very injurious if not fatal for a man of his race to approach too closely or venture a judgment upon it. Further conversing with him to gain an understanding of his ideas, I learned that he considered it quite safe and practicable for a white man to investigate as I was doing, but very hazardous for a black. With this unsatisfactory solution of the mystery, my inquiries ceased, and hunting was resumed.

The Mohammedans have so far remained under the influence of fetishist ideas as to place great confidence in amulets. These are prepared by scholars or instructed men, and consist of verses or words from the Koran. The writing is then folded and sewed into a little leather packet of about two inches square. The packet is tastefully ornamented with geometric or formal designs. It is then hung around the neck by a braided leather cord. Sometimes a really devout person will have half a dozen of these suspended on his breast at once. Baba Djalu, the *patron* of my little barge, had a fine collection of these,

and I had more than one lively conversation, on the
fo'c's'le of the little boat, with respect to their virtues.
He finally gave me one and sold me another at a price
sufficient to cover both articles. This sort of thing, of
course, is very widely spread in the world, and is practiced by Christians as well as by Mohammedans and
fetishists, and also by *soi-disant* enlightened people in
all lands, who make no profession of religion at all.

I here repeat my conviction that Mohammedanism
in the Sudan not only has a future influence which may
surprise the European world and which presents a distinct challenge to Christian missions, but that its influence at the present time is for the good of the
natives. The evils of Islamic belief spring mainly from
the intolerance and fanatical hostility which it breeds.
But the black is not intolerant, and upon his docile and
gentle nature, if he is rightly led, it may be productive
of good.

This brings me, finally, to the subject of political and
religious unrest. The eastern Sudan in modern times
has been the seat of the most startling and vehement
fanatical outbreak which Mohammedanism has occasioned within a century. Mahdism ran its course,
devastated the eastern Sudan, cut down the population
to a fraction of its former strength, then broke, and,
from a military standpoint, was destroyed by the Anglo-
Egyptian forces led into the Sudan by Lord Kitchener.
This British success forced its political center westward, and the Mahdist renegade, Rabah, transferred
the militant spirit of the movement to Lake Chad,
where he overcame the decadent native kingdoms in

the basin of that great lake, and for a time exercised formidable sway. Rabah's power was broken and he himself slain by the French expeditions, under Gentil, which converged upon Lake Chad, in 1898, destroyed this resurgence of Mahdist political power and established the strength of Europe on Lake Chad.

Mahdism, however, still persists, and the spirit of revolt which it represents breaks out in minor rebellions from time to time. The concessions made by the British government in Egypt, just and salutary though they may be, make government in the central Sudan more difficult. Reports of such a matter as Egyptian independence and disaffection at Khartum spread very rapidly, and are widely discussed throughout the Sudan. In all the important towns there are "imams", or religious leaders, who, while living quietly in their own homes, are the recipients of constant intelligence that comes and goes swiftly throughout the breadth of Africa. Each one of these singular men is a center of anti-European feeling, and a focus of future difficulty. One feels this to be truer of Northern Nigeria at the present time than of French West Africa, but the ties that bind together the secret religious orders of the Mohammedan world are intricate, strong, and apparently hard to trace down.

It is not to be presumed that the blacks, conscious though they may be, in a way, of the extraordinary benefits they have received from French and British rule, will remain perpetually content with their subordinate position. Great care, intelligence and patience must be exercised to advance the development of these peoples and not have their progress broken by revolutions and religious convulsions. Success may lie in binding the interests of the more intelligent classes to those of the foreign ruler, until the fortune of a native prince or leader rests upon the permanence of foreign support. This is the British principle. The French proceed in a different way, and expect to hold native attachment, particularly among the influential and more intelligent classes, by inculcating a respect, admiration and even an affection for French culture. In this process the French clearly are proceeding along the lines of imperial Rome. That white rule in the Sudan, both French and British, is beneficent and just, is obvious and beyond disproof. Nowhere in colonial life have the moral qualities of Europe been given finer emphasis than in the relations here established between the white and black races. The prospects of the Sudan rest entirely in the continuation of this authority.

The only question is, Can the black participate and, if so, how far? It is clear that the race, including the mixed stocks, is, in general, deficient in political capacity. Its culture produces only despotisms, and these of a singularly brutal type. The occasional benevolence of a vigorous ruler is quickly succeeded by a record of infamy and bestiality under which political authority is shattered or decays. The arrest of African culture may perhaps be better explained by the political incapacity of the race than by any other intellectual deficiency. The black lacks an inherent passion for freedom, the ability to distinguish between what justly may be demanded of him and what is oppression. No part of the problem of Africa is of more interest than that which has to do with the political competence and aspirations of the native. Because of the present strength of white rule, and not in spite of it, I have a belief that here, in this great area of the Sudan, lie perhaps the best prospects which the African race possesses, and that if striking results are to be hoped for through the influence of European civilization, they will occur here. Few regions of the earth present a more attractive laboratory for the study of the relations between the races than does this Land of the Blacks.

INDEX

Abd-el-Aziz, Sultan, 80
Abd-el-Krim, 33; 50; 55; 68
Abijan, 122; 179
Abyssinia, 8
Adrar, 124; 128; 142
Africa, 3; Assn. for promoting
  discovery of, 4; western A., 7;
  culture, 8; 11; transformation
  of, 19; arts, 80; economic pro-
  duction, 194; 233
Aguedal, 86
Ahaggar, 15; 17; 124; 128
Ahmadu, Almany, 106
Aïr, 125; 126; 142
Akka, 14
Algeria, 15; 23; 25; 26; 27; 55;
  142
Algiers, 13
Alibani, 135
Almohades, 28; 86
Almoravides, 28
Ambidédi, 119
America, citizens in Morocco, 61;
  trade with Morocco, 62; trade
  with Dakar, 111-112; under-
  takings in Tropics, 202-203;
  trade with Gold Coast, 208
American Consuls, 57; 62; 112
Amulets, 241
Anadi Talori, cook, 136; 167
Andalucía, 12; 26
Anderson, Alexander, 4
Arab, 21; 22; 23; 28; 42
Araoan, 148; 151
Arguin, 105
Arms, 97-98; permit for, 109;
  169
Atar, 107
Atlas Mountains, 14; 20; 40; 51
Aube, Lieutenant, 145

Augustine, St., 20
Automobile, Saharan traverse by,
  129-130; Citdöen Co., 130.
Aviation service, Morocco, 44
Azemmour, 45

Baba Djalu, 135; 241
Bamako, 5; 92-93; 106; 119;
  132; 204
Bambara (kingdom and tribe),
  4; 234
Bandiagara, 93; 161
Bani River, 139
Banquet in Morocco, 57-61
Baobab, 119; 165
Barbary, 20; cities of, 25
Barbary Coast, 7; 20
Barka, ex-tirailleur, 168-169
Barth, Dr. Heinrich, 6; 83; 126;
  144-145; 157
Bazin, René, 13
Beni-Abbes, 15; 16; 17
Berbers, 12; 21; nomadic and
  sedentary, 21-22; 23; 24; 25;
  27; 51; 52; 67; 73; 78; 89;
  104; 139; raiders across des-
  ert, 155; 181; 234
Binger, Capt., 177
Blacks, 89; tirailleurs, 91; 104;
  139; employment as soldiers,
  180-187; as civil servants, 221;
  222; 226; representation in
  Senegal, 228-230; 233-245; de-
  meanor, 236; not intolerant,
  242; rule over, 244; political
  participation of, 244-245
Blanc, M., 42-43
Blumenbach, classification of human species, 234
Bobos, 176; 200

247